Cambridge Student

WITHDRAWN

Shakespeare

Romeo and Juliet

Rex Gibson

Series Editor: Rex Gibson

CAMBRIDGE
UNIVERSITY PRESS

PUBLISHED BY THE PRESS SYNDICATE OF THE UNIVERSITY OF CAMBRIDGE
The Pitt Building, Trumpington Street, Cambridge, United Kingdom

CAMBRIDGE UNIVERSITY PRESS
The Edinburgh Building, Cambridge CB2 2RU, UK
40 West 20th Street, New York, NY 10011–4211, USA
477 Williamstown Road, Port Melbourne, VIC 3207, Australia
Ruiz de Alarcón 13, 28014 Madrid, Spain
Dock House, The Waterfront, Cape Town 8001, South Africa

http://www.cambridge.org

First published 2002

Printed in the United Kingdom at the University Press, Cambridge

Typeface 9.5/12pt Scala   *System* QuarkXPress®

A catalogue record for this book is available from the British Library

ISBN 0 521 00813 1 paperback

Cover image: © Getty Images/PhotoDisc

308488

Contents

Introduction   **4**

Commentary   **5**

Contexts   **52**
What did Shakespeare write?   52
What did Shakespeare read?   54
What was Shakespeare's England like?   60
   Feuding and violence   61
   The Elizabethan household and patriarchal authority   61
   Children and sexual maturity   64
   The plague   65
   Religion   66
   Contempt for foreigners   68
   Death   69
Shakespeare's own life   71

Language   **72**
Antithesis   72
Imagery   74
Repetition   77
Lists   79
Verse and prose   81

Critical approaches   **84**
Traditional criticism   84
Modern criticism   89
   Political criticism   90
   Feminist criticism   93
   Performance criticism   97
   Psychoanalytic criticism   101
   Postmodern criticism   102

Organising your responses   **105**
Writing about an extract   106
Writing an essay   114
Writing about character   118
A note on examiners   123

Resources   **124**
Books   124
Films   127
Audio books   128
Romeo and Juliet on the Web   128

Introduction

Romeo and Juliet. The very title conjures up a mental picture of a beautiful young girl on a balcony, with a young man reaching lovingly up towards her. The two names suggest a young couple, head over heels in love, who are destroyed by the implacable enmity of their families. Shakespeare's play is largely responsible for how these familiar images have become part of popular imagination worldwide, symbolising romantic love and doomed lovers.

But *Romeo and Juliet* is far richer and more complex than such images suggest. The action develops with explosive speed. Romeo and Juliet meet, fall instantly in love, and marry the next day. But Romeo is straightway caught up in a bloody encounter: his killing of Tybalt results in his banishment. Juliet is abandoned by her parents and her Nurse and, in a desperate plot to rejoin Romeo, is entombed alive in the Capulet monument. The plan goes terribly wrong and the lovers perish.

Shakespeare tightens dramatic tension as he fills the play with oppositions: Montagues versus Capulets, love versus hate, life versus death, youth versus age. Funeral follows marriage, the bridal bed becomes the death-bed. The ideal of romantic love is continually undermined by the insistence of the Nurse and Mercutio on the physical aspects of sex. The language of the play reflects these oppositions, notably in recurring images of light and dark.

Shakespeare fills the play with dramatic irony: characters are unaware of events or of the real meaning of what is said to them. Tybalt does not know that Romeo has become his kinsman; Mercutio never learns of Juliet's existence. As Capulet promises Juliet to Paris, the audience knows she is at that moment in bed with Romeo. Most cruelly, Romeo, about to kill himself, is unaware that Juliet lives.

In *Romeo and Juliet*, Shakespeare expands traditional notions of tragedy. He includes comic elements and gives the play a domestic setting. Romeo and Juliet are not the conventional characters of tragedy: kings or mighty warriors. They are young, innocent and powerless. But in the portrayal of how their passion and vitality is needlessly destroyed, the play conveys the sense of loss and waste that is at the heart of all tragedy.

Commentary

Act 1 The Prologue

The Prologue is spoken by Chorus, a character who, by theatrical custom, takes no part in the play but introduces it and provides a commentary on the action. Chorus tells that the play will show how the death of two young lovers ends the bitter conflict between their violently feuding families. Chorus' words make clear that the mutual hatred of the families is not the only cause of the lovers' deaths. The description of them as 'star-crossed' suggests that fate will play a part in the tragedy. Their 'misadventured piteous overthrows' hint that unlucky accidents will also contribute to their deaths.

The Prologue is written as a sonnet. Its 14 lines are a reminder that Shakespeare may have written many of his sonnets around the time that he wrote the play. Both the play and the *Sonnets* explore the joys and sorrows of love. The influence of the popularity of sonnets at the time will be seen throughout *Romeo and Juliet*. The language of the play often reflects that of the *Sonnets*: elaborate, formally structured and filled with brilliant imagery.

The Prologue emphatically reminds the audience that they are not watching real life, but a company of actors performing a play. For example, 'our scene' is laid in Verona, and the stage 'traffic' will last for two hours. In some modern stage productions, the Prologue is spoken by Romeo or the Prince. In others, the lines are shared between all the members of the cast. Such practices can involve the theatre audience emotionally and imaginatively, and can also increase the sense of the play's theatricality, In contrast, Baz Luhrmann's film presents Chorus as a television newsreader, a dramatic invention that seems designed to persuade the audience they are watching reality. But however the Prologue is delivered, its language contains continual reminders of the essential theatricality of the play. Chorus ends by directly addressing the audience and assuring them that the actors will try hard to please:

> The which if you with patient ears attend,
> What here shall miss, our toil shall strive to mend. *(lines 13–14)*

Act 1 Scene 1

The scene opens with two servants of Capulet joking together. Sampson boasts of his superiority to any Montague, and of how he will sexually abuse their women. The two men's language is full of sexual suggestiveness: 'stand', 'thrust', 'maidenheads', 'tool', 'weapon'. It seems that Shakespeare is here deliberately emphasising the crudely physical aspect of sex in order to provide a striking contrast with one of the central concerns of the play: the tenderness and mutual regard of the love of Romeo and Juliet. The episode also instantly establishes the deep hostility of the two leading families in Verona: the Montagues and Capulets.

That hostility quickly breaks into open conflict. Sampson bites his thumb at the servants of the Montagues, a gesture which in Elizabethan times was deliberately rude and insulting. Sampson's swaggering bravado conceals a cowardly streak, and he is careful not to start the fight, but then the sight of Tybalt (a Capulet) approaching encourages him to challenge the Montagues. Benvolio (a Montague) tries to stop the developing riot, but the arrival of Tybalt adds fuel to the flames. Tybalt aggressively confronts Benvolio, using language which reveals both his character and the poisonous hatred between the two families:

> What, drawn and talk of peace? I hate the word,
> As I hate hell, all Montagues, and thee.
> Have at thee, coward. *(lines 61–3)*

A furious riot ensues as supporters of the two families join in and citizens try to stop the fight. Capulet and Montague themselves appear, Capulet calling for his sword and Montague insulting him. Both men are restrained by their wives. Lady Capulet appears to mock her husband's fighting ability, suggesting that a crutch would suit him better than a sword. Lady Montague clings to her husband, and he struggles to break free. This first glimpse of women in the play seems to cast them as peacemakers, but in many stagings each woman's hostility to the opposing family is made very evident. In some productions, the women themselves have carried swords.

Only the arrival of Escales, Prince of Verona, stops the brawl, but even he has difficulty in making himself heard at first. He rebukes Montague and Capulet, and threatens death if they fight in public again. His language is formal and elaborate. Bloodstained swords are 'neighbour-stained steel'. Bleeding wounds become 'purple fountains'. The Prince's pun on 'grave' as he describes accessories more appropriate to old men than swords ('grave beseeming ornaments') is one of the play's many subtle reminders of death. Escales' rebuke reveals his impatience that the long-standing feud had its origin in a trivial incident ('bred of an airy word'). It also displays his absolute authority in Verona. He holds the power of life and death over his subjects.

With the departure of the Prince and others, only Benvolio and Montague and his wife are left on stage. Benvolio's account of the riot includes a mocking description of the swordplay of 'the fiery Tybalt'. The conversation then turns to Romeo. Benvolio tells how Romeo has deliberately avoided him, and Montague confirms that Romeo keeps to himself, locking himself away in the darkness of his room, and refusing to say why he behaves so strangely. Benvolio promises to find the cause of Romeo's melancholy. The silence of Lady Montague throughout this episode seems to be another sign of the powerlessness of women in Verona. She has only two lines in which to express her concern for her son. Fathers, rather than mothers, are the dominant parents in the play.

Seeing Romeo approaching, Benvolio urges the Montagues to leave so that he may discover the cause of his friend's melancholy. Romeo says his sadness is caused by love. Rosaline (whom he does not name) will not return his love. The sight of the signs of the riot prompts him to a long series of oxymorons (two contradictory words brought together to create a striking expression): 'loving hate', 'heavy lightness', 'feather of lead' and others. Oxymoron was a popular language device in the love poetry of Shakespeare's time. Here, it serves two purposes: first, to convey Romeo's contradictory emotions of love; second, to embody the conflicts at the heart of the play. Just as Capulet is set against Montague, so in each oxymoron the word is set against the word: 'love' against 'hate' and so on. The tension of the drama is reflected and expressed in the language itself. But Romeo seems more interested in the conflicts of love than of the feuding families: he goes on to characterise love in another ˟ of oppositions which end with:

> What is it else? a madness most discreet,
> A choking gall, and a preserving sweet.

8
Commentary

The play's link with the *Sonnets* is evident as Romeo despairs that Rosaline (again, not named) is sworn to chastity, and so will leave no children. The theme of dying childless is a preoccupation of the *Sonnets*. There are further echoes of the love poetry of the time in Romeo's praise of Rosaline's beauty. Many critics have argued that Romeo's elaborate language, full of fanciful imagery and rhyming couplets, shows that his love is not sincere, but is merely infatuation. His emotions for Rosaline are as artificial as his language. Perhaps Benvolio suspects as much when he claims the cure for Romeo's problem is simply to look at other girls. But Romeo is not convinced.

Act 1 Scene 2

The scene opens in the middle of a conversation between Capulet and Paris (a relative of Prince Escales). The Prince has ordered both Capulet and Montague to keep the peace. Paris regrets that the two men have been such long-standing enemies, but then asks for Capulet's response to his wish to marry Juliet. Capulet's reply reveals three ways in which Shakespeare prepares to intensify the drama's effect on the audience: Juliet's age, Capulet's character, and the invitations to Capulet's party. Juliet is revealed to be only 13, an age which Elizabethans considered far too young for marriage (see page 64). Capulet's other children have died ('Earth hath swallowed all my hopes but she'), so all his affection will be centred on his sole surviving daughter. He thinks Paris should wait at least two more years, but says that if Juliet consents, he will agree. This impression of Capulet as a caring, considerate father will stand in stark contrast to his later behaviour. Finally, Capulet's despatch of a servant to invite guests to a party ('feast') that night is the action that will set the plot moving towards its tragic end.

The servant is illiterate, and so looks for someone to read the names of the invited guests to him. He meets Romeo, who is again being advised by Benvolio to look at other girls to cure his love for Rosaline ('one fire burns out another's burning'). Romeo reads the list, discovers Rosaline's name on it, then learns that the party's host is Capulet – the sworn enemy of all Montagues. Benvolio urges Romeo to go to the party, where he will see women more beautiful than Rosaline. Romeo agrees to go, but denies that any woman could match Rosaline's beauty. Shakespeare's stagecraft is evident in the ʾisode: he leaves it entirely to the actors to decide how to react to

Rosaline's name on the list, and to the news that the party is at Capulet's home, where Montagues are not welcome. His use of contemporary events is also evident. In Romeo's elaborate image claiming that his eyes would burn out if he saw someone more beautiful than Rosaline, Shakespeare is drawing upon the cruel sixteenth-century practice of burning religious disbelievers ('heretics') at the stake:

> Transparent heretics, be burnt for liars.   *(line 91)*

Act 1 Scene 3

After two scenes dominated by males, the dramatic focus now shifts to the three major female characters, and shows them to be very different in personality and language. Lady Capulet and the Nurse discuss Juliet's age. Their repeated insistence that 'She's not fourteen' suggests Shakespeare's concern to impress upon his audience Juliet's youth and vulnerability. That impression is strengthened by the few lines that she speaks in the scene. Six of her seven lines suggest she is submissive and compliant, but because performance allows for very different tones of speaking, a very different impression of her character can be conveyed. For example, her very first words, 'How now, who calls?' have sometimes been spoken resentfully and defiantly.

The Nurse's language is quite distinct from other speech styles in the play. Actresses who play the part eagerly seize the opportunities Shakespeare offers to create a memorable stage character. The Nurse is earthy and longwinded. Her rambling story of Juliet's infancy is full of sexual innuendo as she recalls her husband's joke about Juliet's future sexuality. Whether Juliet fully understands the Nurse's meaning is open for each production to decide. Sometimes she is portrayed on stage as clearly baffled by the Nurse's joke that she will 'fall backward'. In one production, her sexual inexperience was conveyed by having her playing with a doll, not hearing all that the Nurse says. It is usual for the Nurse to convey the sense of a warm and close relationship with Juliet, and her lines recalling her own dead daughter can create a poignant moment, touching the audience's feelings:

> Well, Susan is with God,
> She was too good for me.   *(lines 20–1)*

How Lady Capulet responds to the Nurse is open to a wide range of stage performance. Sometimes she is obviously irritated, showing she thinks the Nurse to be tedious and garrulous. More often she displays friendly tolerance, showing the Nurse to be an accepted and trusted member of the Capulet household. But whatever the relationship suggested, Lady Capulet seizes upon the Nurse's wish to see Juliet married, using it as her opportunity to talk about Paris' proposal of marriage. Her lines contain another reminder of Juliet's age, and the revelation that Lady Capulet, like other high-status females in Verona, became a mother at 13 or younger. Once again, Shakespeare is emphasising the difference between his fictional Italian society and the experience of his audience. Elizabethan mothers were typically much older (see pages 64–5).

Lady Capulet's praise of Paris is delivered in rhyming couplets. Her 14 sonnet-like lines elaborately compare Paris to an expensively bound book. Such fanciful and imaginative analogies (known as 'conceits') were popular in the poetry of the time, and Elizabethans valued their inventiveness highly. But most modern critics do not share that estimate, and consider Lady Capulet's lines to be artificial and insincere. They judge the comparison as incongruous and confused, and the rhythm and rhyme as mechanical and forced. The Nurse, in typical fashion, turns Lady Capulet's final couplet into a joke about pregnancy: 'bigger women grow by men'. In sharp contrast, Juliet seems dutiful and obedient. She uses the image of Cupid's arrow ('dart') to say that the way she looks at Paris will be guided by what her mother advises:

> But no more deep will I endart mine eye
> Than your consent gives strength to make it fly.   *(lines 99–100)*

Act 1 Scene 4

Juliet ended the previous scene with the image of Cupid, the god of love. That image is strongly developed as Romeo and his friends, carrying masks and torches, prepare for their visit to Capulet's party. Benvolio rejects any idea of disguise as Cupid carrying a bow, and Mercutio tries to laugh Romeo out of his sadness by telling him to soar on Cupid's wings. Romeo replies he is so pierced by Cupid's arrow that he cannot be lighthearted. Love makes him sad. Shakespeare adds variety to the play's love theme by having the young men use puns, a fashionable device of the love poetry of the time: 'measure', 'soles', 'bound', 'prick' and 'visor' are all punned upon. At this moment there is no mention of the feud or the danger of entering the home of the Montagues' enemy. Love is the subject of the scene's opening.

Romeo's melancholy mood persists. He has no wish to join in the dancing. Mercutio continues his efforts to tease Romeo out of his low spirits. He seizes on Romeo's claim that dreams contain truth, and embarks on a long account of Queen Mab, the fairy who causes humans to dream. He describes the intricate detail of her coach, and tells of the dreams she creates in the minds of all kinds of sleepers: lovers, courtiers, lawyers, churchmen, soldiers and others.

Mercutio's tale of Queen Mab has become a famous 'recitation piece', and it can seem merely a flight of fancy by Shakespeare, holding up the action for a long moment of superbly imaginative poetry. But the speech is significant for at least three major reasons. First, it gives insight into Shakespeare's own times. It is Shakespeare's adaptation or parody of all kinds of superstitions, folk tales, myths and stereotypical characters popular in Elizabethan England. Second, it functions dramatically to intensify the love theme of the play and to heighten the impression of Romeo's isolation: the difference of his mood from his friends. Third, the speech reveals much about Mercutio, and gives actors dazzling opportunities to create their own version of the character.

Even though Mercutio declares that dreams are 'the children of an idle brain', the Queen Mab speech reveals his own brain to be far from idle. It shows Mercutio to be witty and highly inventive. His imagination soars as he piles up fantasy on fantasy in dream-like switches from one vivid creation to the next. Some actors deliver the speech as a drug-induced illusion. Others portray Mercutio as dangerously near to madness or frenzy, his mind caught up in an ever-increasing spiral of free association. In a quite different character portrayal, in one production Mercutio took Romeo on his knee and spoke the speech like a kindly father telling a bedtime story to a three-year-old. All these very different portrayals can be theatrically valid.

But the scene ends on an ominous note. All Mercutio's joking and fantasising have not lightened Romeo's mood. He expresses fearful unease, and prophesies that his own premature ('untimely') death will result from attending 'this night's revels' at Capulet's feast. Even though he puts his life in the hands of God, and determines to go along with the others, his language conveys a sense of deep foreboding, and echoes the Prologue's description of 'A pair of star-crossed lovers', fated to die:

> my mind misgives
> Some consequence yet hanging in the stars   *(lines 106–7)*

Act 1 Scene 5

Shakespeare chooses to begin the scene in Capulet's house with servants preparing the room for dancing. In a short bustling episode of only 14 lines, the audience gains a glimpse into what goes on 'below stairs'. It is usually performed to bring out the humour in the scene, but dramatically it reflects some of the tensions and preoccupations of the play: Potpan is accused of neglecting his duty, the First Servant looks forward to sexual pleasure with Susan Grindstone and Nell, and the Fourth Servant's proverb carries an echo of premature death ('the longer liver take all'). Just as Shakespeare began the play with servants expressing the antagonism of their masters, so the opening of Scene 5 also shows how the interests of the low-status people of Verona echo those of the leading citizens.

Capulet welcomes his guests. He seems the traditional jovial host as he addresses the women with literally 'corny' jokes and tells the men how successfully he could flirt in his youth. He acts as a master of ceremonies, despatching good-natured orders to the musicians, dancers and servants. On stage, many actors present Capulet as a mellow, pleasant character as he reminisces with his cousin about their 'dancing days', now long past. His language suggests that he is considerably older than his wife, who implied in Scene 3 that she is not yet 30.

Shakespeare provides only very brief stage directions in the scene: 'Music plays'; 'And they dance'. He gives no indication of how Romeo and his friends are behaving, or what Juliet is doing. Some stage productions present the festivities in dazzling style, and the Baz Luhrmann film makes it extravagantly spectacular. But however strikingly the dancing or other entertainment is performed, the audience's attention must be made to focus on Romeo, and his reaction to his first sight of Juliet. All productions attempt, in very different ways, to maximise the dramatic impact of his question to a servant, and his first comment on Juliet:

ROMEO   What lady's that which doth enrich the hand
              Of yonder knight?
SERVINGMAN   I know not, sir.
ROMEO   O she doth teach the torches to burn bright!   *(lines 40–3)*

It is love at first sight. Romeo is entranced by Juliet's beauty, and describes her in elaborate imagery. He dismisses all thoughts of Rosaline ('Did my heart love till now?') and declares 'I ne'er saw true beauty till this night'. Shakespeare gives the actor a difficult task. Romeo's affections have switched in an instant from Rosaline to Juliet, but he must convey to the audience that his love for Juliet is not infatuation. Every production of the play works out in detail just how Romeo and Juliet first glimpse each other, and how they behave before they speak together. In Baz Luhrmann's film, their eyes meet as they gaze wonderingly through a fish tank.

At this very moment of falling in love, Shakespeare tightens dramatic tension. Tybalt explodes with rage as he hears Romeo's voice. He is outraged that a Montague should dare gatecrash Capulet's party, and seems set on killing him. Once again Capulet is shown in a favourable light. He praises Romeo ('a virtuous and well-governed youth') and rebukes Tybalt fiercely and contemptuously. Tybalt threatens vengeance as he leaves. His ominous antithesis (see page 72) reminds the audience of the dangers that lie in wait for the two young lovers:

                    this intrusion shall,
Now seeming sweet, convert to bitt'rest gall.   *(lines 90–1)*

Shakespeare again switches the mood of the scene. He writes Romeo and Juliet's first conversation as a sonnet. Sonnets were the most popular type of love poetry at the time Shakespeare wrote the play, so the form of the lines, as well as their content, speaks of love. The sonnet is full of religious imagery ('profane', 'holy shrine', 'sin', 'pilgrims' and so on), which some critics interpret as symbolising the purity and sincerity of Romeo and Juliet's love. Stagings of the encounter try to bring out its tenderness, but also try to suggest the depth of passion that Romeo and Juliet feel for each other, but cannot openly show. It is the choice of each actress playing Juliet to decide whether to make her words after their second kiss ('You kiss by th'book') sound like a rebuke, a compliment, a surprised comment, or some other reaction.

The Nurse calls Juliet away, and Romeo learns that she is the daughter of his family's deadly enemy. As the party breaks up, Juliet also learns Romeo's identity: 'The only son of your great enemy'. Her response, framed in the antitheses (opposing words, e.g. 'only love' – 'only hate') that so often express the conflicts in the play, ominously foreshadows the tragedy to come:

> My only love sprung from my only hate!
> Too early seen unknown, and known too late!
> Prodigious birth of love it is to me,
> That I must love a loathèd enemy. *(lines 137–40)*

Act 1 Chorus

Chorus began the play with a sonnet spoken to the audience. Now Chorus speaks another sonnet which, in its summary of the action so far and introduction of the next scene, is a further reminder that the audience is watching a play, not real life. The sonnet tells that Romeo's infatuation with Rosaline has ended and he now loves Juliet, who returns his love. These 14 lines are often cut in production. Critics do not value the sonnet highly, and often repeat Doctor Johnson's claim that it adds nothing to the audience's understanding and gives no insight into the play's moral issues. But it is significant that both the content and the imagery of the sonnet are sinister reminders of the dangers lying ahead for the young couple. Their families' enmity makes each a 'foe' to the other, and Juliet must now 'steal love's sweet bait from fearful hooks'.

Act 1: Critical review

Act 1 establishes the two-fold strife that will run through the play: the conflict of hate and the conflict of love. The hate that pervades Verona is all too evident. The first scene explodes into violent conflict between the Montagues and Capulets, and the last scene shows Tybalt angrily vowing to take vengeance on Romeo for daring to intrude into the Capulet festivities.

The conflicts of love take different forms in the Act. Most obvious is the discovery made by Romeo and Juliet in the final minutes of Scene 5. They have just fallen deeply in love, but now they find they are the children of deadly enemies: 'My only love sprung from my only hate!' The baleful influence of the feud instantly clouds their joy.

But Shakespeare also enacts other conflicts of love in the opening Act. He contrasts infatuation with true love, setting Romeo's synthetic feelings for Rosaline against his genuine love for Juliet. Romeo is first shown in love with the fashionable literary idea of love, and he expresses his affection in the language of conventional romance. Meeting Juliet exposes the artificiality and insincerity of such bookish notions of love.

Just as striking is the contrast of love with sex. The Nurse and Mercutio joke obsessively about sex. They will continue to do so in every future appearance. Their insistent reminders of the sexual act constantly undermine and challenge the ideal of romantic love.

Act 1 emphasises Juliet's youth and vulnerability. Shakespeare makes her only 13, an age which Elizabethans thought far too young for marriage. He also shows how closely her father and mother control her life, both actively concerned that she should marry Paris. The dramatic effect is to create suspense: whilst her parents think of her as the future bride of the man they favour, she has fallen in love with the son of their enemy.

The Act also provides evidence that the tragedy is not simply rooted in the feud. There are recurring reminders of the malign influence of fate, for example as the Prologue speaks of 'star-crossed lovers' and Romeo fears 'Some consequence yet hanging in the stars'. But Shakespeare's choosing to begin and end the Act with Chorus reminds the audience that they are watching a play, not real life.

ortly after Capulet's party has ended. Romeo has broken
is friends, who are now seeking him. Mercutio mocks
vesickness, pretending to be a magician raising up spirits
conjure too'). Mercutio believes that Romeo is still in love
with Rosaline, and his ridicule is filled with sexual innuendo about
her. The scene strengthens the impression of Mercutio's brilliant
inventiveness and his readiness to exploit the sexual implications of
every situation. It also develops the love theme of the play. Mercutio's
preoccupation with the merely physical aspects of love contrasts
strongly with the sincerity of the love of Romeo and Juliet.

The scene is also important for what it suggests about Elizabethan
staging practices. Benvolio says that Romeo has 'leapt this orchard
wall', but it is very unlikely that in Shakespeare's time a wall was
brought on stage. Shakespeare parodied that practice in the
Mechanicals' play in *A Midsummer Night's Dream*, in which Snout the
tinker appears in loam and roughcast as Wall. On the bare stage of an
Elizabethan theatre, Romeo probably hid behind a pillar, or stood at
the side of the stage. As usual in Shakespeare's plays, the location of
a scene is suggested by the language. Here, Benvolio's words imply
that the next scene will find Romeo in Capulet's orchard.

Act 2 Scene 2

'He jests at scars that never felt a wound.' Romeo's first line is a
dismissive comment on Mercutio's joking about love. Just as someone
who has never been wounded can jest about a soldier's battle scars, so
someone who has never been in love finds it easy to joke about the
sufferings of a person deeply in love. Many actors speak the line wryly
or ironically, rather than bitterly, to suggest that although Romeo
criticises Mercutio their friendship is still intact. But, as he catches
sight of Juliet at a window of the house, his next two lines and the rest
of his first speech require the actor to express Romeo's unqualified
love for Juliet:

> But soft, what light through yonder window breaks?
> It is the east, and Juliet is the sun. *(lines 2–3)*

Scene 2 is known as the 'balcony' scene, even though Shakespeare
does not use the word 'balcony' and provides no such stage direction.

Romeo's many comparisons of Juliet to the sun, stars and heavens suggest that he is looking upwards, and that Juliet appears at an upstairs window. The tradition of a balcony has arisen from stage practice in which, until recent times, it was often realistically presented. But whatever the physical setting of the meeting of the lovers, the intensity of their language creates a lyrical, passionate mood. The first 50 lines are virtually soliloquies, but the scene is often described in musical terms as a 'love-duet', because each has the other so ardently in mind.

Romeo describes Juliet as the source of light itself. When she first speaks, he uses religious images of adoration, comparing her to an angel, 'a wingèd messenger of heaven' upon whom mortals fall back to gaze upon in wonder. Shakespeare sets this very personal moment in the dramatic context of the feud: unaware of Romeo's presence, Juliet shows she is fully conscious of the hatred that makes their families deadly enemies. Why should he be called Romeo, she asks, a Montague – the implacable rivals of the Capulets? She declares her love, recognising that only his name is her enemy, not Romeo himself. He is what he is, whatever his name, just as a rose is naturally fragrant, whatever it is called:

> O be some other name!
> What's in a name? That which we call a rose
> By any other word would smell as sweet.   *(lines 42–4)*

Juliet's admission of love prompts Romeo to reveal himself, and to declare his hate for his name. She fears for his safety. He will be killed if he is discovered. But Romeo dismisses the danger. Neither stone walls nor the Capulet kinsmen can prevent his love. Juliet's love and the cover of night protect him. In an image which will recur dramatically in his final speech in the play, Romeo compares himself to a sea-voyager driven to seek Juliet's love, even if it were at the very ends of the earth:

> I am no pilot, yet wert thou as far
> As that vast shore washed with the farthest sea,
> I should adventure for such merchandise.   *(lines 82–4)*

Juliet admits embarrassment at being overheard telling of her love. She rejects formal ways of speaking and behaving ('farewell compliment') and asks Romeo directly if he loves her. She pleads with him to answer truthfully ('pronounce it faithfully'), admitting she declared her own love for him unaware of his presence. She begs him not to swear his love by the moon, which is changeable and inconstant, but only by himself. Suddenly fearful, she sees their instant falling in love as 'too rash, too unadvised'. It may prove as brief as a lightning flash, over as quickly as it began. In reply to Romeo's anxious question why she wishes to withdraw her vow of love and offer it again, Juliet uses simple but profoundly eloquent language to expresses the never-ending quality of her love for him:

> My bounty is as boundless as the sea,
> My love as deep; the more I give to thee
> The more I have, for both are infinite.   *(lines 133–5)*

Juliet briefly leaves, called by the Nurse, and Romeo fears he is simply dreaming. Juliet returns, promising marriage, and saying she will send a messenger tomorrow to learn the place and time of the wedding. Shakespeare increases the dramatic effect of the lovers' exchanges, adding urgency and tension as the Nurse's calls interrupt Juliet's plea for Romeo not to be false. She leaves again, and Romeo compares lovers' meetings and farewells to the joy or sorrow with which schoolboys go from or towards school (an image Shakespeare would later use in the 'seven ages of man' speech in *As You Like It*: 'creeping like snail / Unwillingly to school').

Juliet returns again and calls Romeo back. She declares that like a prisoner she must whisper ('Bondage is hoarse'). Feminist critics in particular have argued that her words hint at the lack of freedom she has in her father's house. She promises to send the Nurse to Romeo the next morning, and in a moment that can be staged for laughter or for poignancy, she declares 'I have forgot why I did call thee back'. Productions sometimes follow the line with a long period of silent wonder as the two lovers look at each other without speaking. Some critics see this moment as the climax of the scene, where the lovers attain a perfect communion in silence. It is a statement of love that needs no words.

The scene ends with Romeo leaving to seek Friar Lawrence's help. But, just as Juliet has played the dominant role in the scene (she speaks twice as many lines as Romeo), it is her farewell that often remains in the audience's mind as the memorable expression of lovers' leave-taking. She ends with an oxymoron that encapsulates the conflicts of the play and its joys and heartaches:

> Parting is such sweet sorrow *(line 184)*

Act 2 Scene 3

It is daybreak, and Friar Lawrence is gathering flowers and herbs. In a few productions, his first four lines are spoken by Romeo at the end of the previous scene (for the reason given on page 53). Friar Lawrence is a Franciscan, a religious order famous in Elizabethan times for its medical knowledge and healing power. The Friar's knowledge will later play a crucial part in the tragedy, and here Shakespeare prepares the audience as Lawrence meditates that the plants he collects contain both healing medicine and poison. They can both cure and kill. The Friar's final selection of one 'weak flower' that 'stays all senses with the heart' will return in Act 4 with tragic consequences for the young lovers.

Friar Lawrence's frequent use of antithesis (opposing words) expresses the contrasting powers of good and bad contained within the flowers: 'day' versus 'night', 'baleful weeds' versus 'precious-juiced flowers', 'mother' versus 'grave', 'tomb' versus 'womb', 'vile' versus 'good', 'fair use' versus 'abuse', 'virtue' versus 'vice'. The many antitheses reflect the Christian view of nature: its capacity for both good and evil. Elizabethan Christians also saw that dual potential for excellence and corruption in human beings. Friar Lawrence summarises those views as he contrasts the divine virtue ('grace') that humankind possesses with the destructive effects of human passions ('rude will'):

> Two such opposèd kings encamp them still
> In man as well as herbs, grace and rude will *(lines 27–8)*

Prompted by Romeo's appearance so early in the morning, Friar Lawrence continues his moralising style of rhyming couplets. He fears Romeo has spent the night with Rosaline. Romeo's elaborate reply, also in rhyming couplets, appeals for the Friar's help. Once again Shakespeare reminds the audience of the Christian setting of the play as Friar Lawrence finds Romeo's explanation ambiguous and unsatisfactory. As a Franciscan priest, Friar Lawrence could give absolution ('shrift' = pardon) to those who confessed their sins to him. Lawrence asks Romeo to speak more plainly, because 'Riddling confession finds but riddling shrift': unsatisfactory confession will receive only imperfect forgiveness.

Romeo obeys the Friar's command to tell his story clearly: he and Juliet are in love, and he wants the Friar to marry them. Friar Lawrence delays his consent, rebuking Romeo for his fickleness in love. Once again he uses rhyming couplets to moralise, using the signs of Romeo's previous love (tears, sighs, groans) to generalise on men's unfaithfulness. When Romeo responds that the Friar had earlier ordered him to bury his love for Rosaline, Lawrence's rebuke, although its image has sinister undertones, often evokes audience laughter:

Not in a grave,
To lay one in, another out to have.   *(lines 83–4)*

Friar Lawrence agrees to marry Romeo and Juliet because he believes that their marriage will end the feuding of the Montagues and Capulets. Romeo urges haste, but the Friar's final line, yet another moralising generalisation, ominously predicts that the speed of the lovers' romance will lead to disaster:

Wisely and slow, they stumble that run fast.   *(line 94)*

Act 2 Scene 4

Romeo's friends are still unaware of his new-found love for Juliet. Mercutio jokes with Benvolio about Romeo's infatuation with Rosaline, but Benvolio has disquieting news: Tybalt has challenged Romeo to a duel. Mercutio laughs off the challenge and mocks Tybalt's precise style of sword-fencing. His ridicule reveals much about the fashionable styles of fighting and speaking practised by many young aristocrats of Shakespeare's day. Mercutio scornfully pokes fun at the Italian terms to be found in sword-fencing manuals ('passado', 'punto reverso') and derides the affected accents and catch phrases of 'phantasimes', posturing dandies: 'By Jesu, a very good blade!' and so on.

Nonetheless, Mercutio's joking about swords acknowledges the very real danger of Tybalt's challenge. Elizabethan audiences would recognise the same menacing undercurrent in Mercutio's humorous greeting of Romeo. He teases Romeo about his love, accusing him of writing love poetry ('numbers') to Rosaline like that of the fourteenth-century Italian poet Petrarch to his love, Laura (see page 57). But all the examples Mercutio gives are ominous, because all ended tragically:

- *Dido* queen of Carthage. She killed herself when her lover Aeneas deserted her.
- *Cleopatra* queen of Egypt. After the suicide of her lover Mark Antony, she also killed herself.
- *Helen* wife of Menelaus, king of Sparta, was stolen by the Trojan Prince, Paris. Her abduction led to the siege and destruction of Troy.
- *Hero* Every night her lover Leander swam across the Hellespont (the Dardanelles) to meet her. He drowned.
- *Thisbe* loved Pyramus. Their families were bitter enemies. The two lovers committed suicide, unable to live without each other.

But Romeo is in high spirits, and the two young friends joke together, each trying to outdo each other's puns. Their dialogue is highly elaborate and artificial, and full of bawdy (sexual meanings). These showy and fanciful exchanges were much enjoyed in the 1590s: audiences considered such wordplay highly witty. Today, the language makes great demands on actors, because although similar 'joshing' among young men is commonplace, its content is very different. The style is recognisable, but the detailed meaning of Mercutio's and Romeo's language is no longer familiar ('pink', 'pump', 'goose', 'cheverel', etc.). But the episode is highly significant. It reinforces the audience's sense of the closeness and warmth of the two men's relationship. Further, it continues to deepen an important thematic contrast as Mercutio's emphasis on the physical aspect of love opposes the ideal of romantic love.

When the Nurse appears, seeking Romeo, Mercutio directs his sexual teasing at her. Shakespeare seems to invite actors to invent all kinds of stage business (actions to accompany the language), most obviously in Mercutio's 'the bawdy hand of the dial is now upon the prick of noon'. The song he sings may baffle contemporary audiences, but for the Elizabethans it was full of familiar indecencies about prostitution. The Nurse obviously recognises them, as she asks who was this 'saucy merchant' so full of his 'ropery' (dirty jokes). In each production the Nurse must decide how she will react to Mercutio's jibes, and her response has been played in very different ways, from outraged propriety to flattered flirting.

The Nurse warns Romeo not to deceive Juliet ('lead her in a fool's paradise'). He tells her to prepare Juliet to be married that afternoon at Friar Lawrence's cell. He will send a rope ladder to the Nurse so that he may climb into Juliet's room in Capulet's house. The Nurse's language is typically rambling, but her affection for Juliet is evident. Her story that Paris lays claim to Juliet ('would fain lay knife aboard') recalls an Elizabethan custom in which a guest would bring his own knife to claim a place at the table. The story offers opportunities for the actors to give the audience insight into the characters of both Romeo and the Nurse. Shakespeare does not show how Romeo reacts to the news of Paris' intentions: the actor must decide. Sometimes the Nurse turns her report of Juliet's reaction ('as lieve see a toad') and her subsequent teasing of Juliet into an opportunity to ingratiate herself with Romeo. The actress's behaviour can suggest to the audience that the Nurse is lying, adapting what she says to the circumstances of the moment. But it is an equally valid interpretation to perform these lines in a way that suggests she is truthful and sincere.

Act 2 Scene 5

Juliet is waiting impatiently for the Nurse's return. The Nurse had left at nine, but it is now noon. Juliet's soliloquy adds to the sense of the play's gathering speed. It is full of images of the swiftness of young love ('ten times faster', 'nimble-pinioned doves', 'wind-swift Cupid'). The many words that suggest movement ('send', 'return', 'glides', etc.) build up an increasing sense of urgency and anticipation which is frustrated by the slow and heavy pace of 'old folks'. The soliloquy reflects the structure of the rest of the scene that follows, which heightens both dramatic tension and comedy by contrasting Juliet's impatient desire with the Nurse's delaying tactics.

The Nurse arrives, grumbling about her aches and pains. Juliet is eager for news, fearful that the Nurse's sour expression bodes ill. She implores the Nurse to speak, but her eager questions receive only irrelevant replies and another catalogue of the Nurse's aches. The way the Nurse plays on Juliet's frustration is usually a highly comic episode, which climaxes at the moment when she finally seems about to reveal Romeo's news but abruptly switches to a question: 'Where is your mother?'

The Nurse delays a little further but, at last, Juliet hears the longed-for news: Romeo waits to marry her at Friar Lawrence's cell. Promising to collect the rope ladder, the Nurse cannot resist making sexual jokes as she sends Juliet off to her marriage. Juliet's joyous and high-spirited final line will prove dramatically ironic as the play unfolds. Neither her fortune nor the Nurse will prove to be how she describes them:

> Hie to high fortune! Honest Nurse, farewell. *(line 77)*

Act 2 Scene 6

In Friar Lawrence's cell, Romeo and the Friar await Juliet. Friar Lawrence seems confident that heaven will bless the marriage and so prevent future sorrows, and Romeo longs for marriage. But in performance the Friar sometimes delivers his lines nervously, evidently aware of the dangers of marrying the children of deadly enemies. There is a similarly ominous tone in Romeo's assertion that the joy of just one minute of Juliet's love outweighs all that 'love-devouring Death' can do. The mood of lurking menace is deepened as Friar Lawrence anticipates the hazards that can come from joyous love and too hasty action. Like fire meeting gunpowder, passion destroys itself:

> These violent delights have violent ends *(line 9)*

The mood lightens with Juliet's entry. The Friar praises her in a delicate image of lovers seeming to float on air. Romeo uses elaborate language to invite her to give an ornate description ('blazon') of their happiness:

> Ah, Juliet, if the measure of thy joy
> Be heaped like mine, and that thy skill be more
> To blazon it, then sweeten with thy breath
> This neighbour air, and let rich music's tongue
> Unfold the imagined happiness that both
> Receive in either by this dear encounter. *(lines 24–9)*

But Juliet argues that her true love does not need words. It is so rich, it cannot be measured or fully described. Her lines recall her earlier speech 'My bounty is as boundless as the sea' (Act 2 Scene 2, lines 133–5) and anticipate the way Shakespeare would later express the same thought in *Antony and Cleopatra*: 'There's beggary in the love that can be reckoned'. Friar Lawrence clearly recognises the physical desire that lies behind each lover's very different way of speaking. He leads them away to marry, and so make the sexual consummation of their love legitimate in the eyes of the church:

> Come, come with me, and we will make short work,
> For by your leaves, you shall not stay alone
> Till Holy Church incorporate two in one. *(lines 35–7)*

Act 2: Critical review

Act 2 gives the impression of the play gathering speed. It begins with Romeo outside Capulet's house, and ends only hours later with Friar Lawrence leading the lovers away to their marriage. In no more than a day Romeo and Juliet have met, fallen passionately in love, and married. The sheer speed of events stands in ironic contrast to the Friar's advice: 'Wisely and slow, they stumble that run fast'.

The Friar fails to take his own advice. Hearing of Romeo's love for Juliet he quickly agrees to marry the couple, believing their union may end the feuding of the Montagues and Capulets. But just before the ceremony he again acknowledges the dangers of all-consuming passion: 'These violent delights have violent ends'. His ominous words could serve for an emblem for the menace that characterises the Act: Juliet is all too aware that Romeo faces death in the Capulet orchard; the flowers the Friar gathers contain poison; Tybalt's letter challenges Romeo to a duel; the ladies that Mercutio lists are all caught up in tragic stories; and Romeo defies 'love-devouring Death'.

At the heart of the Act is the lyricism of the 'balcony' scene. It shows Juliet speaking plainly and directly from the heart, and Romeo gradually breaking away from the conventional and artificial language of love that he has earlier used about Rosaline. Images of light sparkle throughout the scene, and the constant reminders of night both heighten their brilliance and provide a disturbing contrast.

Romeo and Juliet's love sharply reveals how people in Verona are divided by mere words. Simply being a Capulet or a Montague is cause for enmity. The arbitrariness of such division is recognised in Scene 2 by Juliet when she asks 'What's in a name?' and by Romeo when he offers to tear his name. However, the continual shadow of the feud is a reminder that in Verona people cannot be judged as they are, but by the clan to which they belong.

The close male bonding displayed in Scenes 1 and 4 suggests yet another social constraint on personal authenticity. It reveals itself in the irony of Mercutio's remark 'Now art thou Romeo': an assertion that only in sexual joking is Romeo truly himself. But, as the audience has witnessed, Romeo's language in the 'balcony' scene denies such a narrow and chauvinist view of what it is to be a man.

Act 3 Scene 1

Shakespeare sets the scene in the open air. His language creates a sense of heat and tension as Benvolio fears meeting the Capulets, knowing a fight will surely follow. Mercutio laughs at his fears, accusing Benvolio of being quick-tempered, always looking for a quarrel. He details five examples of the trivial matters over which Benvolio has picked a fight. In the light of what the play has shown of the characters so far, Mercutio's description fits himself better than Benvolio.

Shakespeare reinforces that probability in his choice of the characters' names. As Mercutio's cascading prose leaps from unlikely example to unlikely example, his language suggests his mercurial imagination and nature. In contrast, Benvolio's name loosely translates as 'good-wishing' (just as Malvolio in *Twelfth Night* is 'ill-wishing'). In the very first scene of the play Benvolio had tried to stop the fight between the servants of the Montagues and Capulets. Now he again seeks to avoid conflict, but the entry of Tybalt and servants of the Capulets dooms that hope.

Mercutio taunts Tybalt, clearly wanting to provoke him. He goads Tybalt, seizing on his words and repeating them back with a changed, insulting meaning. But Tybalt, intent on seeking Romeo, ignores each jibe. Benvolio again attempts to keep the peace, but he too is ignored. Romeo enters, and Tybalt challenges him to fight, calling him 'villain' and 'Boy', both deeply offensive terms in the male honour code. Romeo, newly married to Juliet, tries to make peace with Tybalt, who is now his kinsman. He cannot reveal his marriage, but twice suggests he now has good reason for not fighting with the Capulets. Romeo's refusal to fight angers Mercutio, who now challenges Tybalt, mocking his nickname ('Alla stoccata' = rapier thrust):

> O calm, dishonourable, vile submission!
> 'Alla stoccata' carries it away. (*Draws*)
> Tybalt, you rat-catcher, will you walk?   (*lines 66–8*)

Romeo tries desperately to prevent the two men fighting, reminding them that Prince Escales has forbidden such public brawling. But his well-meaning intervention has a fatal result. He steps between the two men and, in the confusion, Tybalt mortally wounds Mercutio, then flees. The following episode is often played to maximise the poignancy of Mercutio's death by having his friends not realise at first how badly wounded he is. Mercutio himself describes his wound as a scratch, and, close to death, cannot resist a punning joke: 'Ask for me tomorrow, and you shall find me a grave man'. Romeo and the others finally grasp how seriously their friend is hurt as Mercutio is helped off, cursing Montagues and Capulets alike:

> A plague a'both your houses!
> They have made worms' meat of me. I have it,
> And soundly too. Your houses!　　　　　　*(lines 97–9)*

Romeo blames himself for Mercutio's wound. Resentful of Tybalt's insults, he fears that his love for Juliet has weakened his courage. Benvolio's report of Mercutio's death shocks Romeo. It also seems intended to shock the audience, too. Why should Shakespeare kill off the most charismatic character when the play has barely reached its half-way point? All kinds of reasons have been put forward (see page 35), but the effect is to ensure that the dramatic focus is now only on Romeo and Juliet, and that the drama is set on an inevitable tragic course: Mercutio's death prompts Romeo to revenge.

Hearing of Mercutio's death, Romeo uses the language of revenge tragedy, the most popular genre of drama in the early 1590s (see pages 58–9). He predicts that the evil outcomes of this day's violence lie in the future: 'This day's black fate on moe (more) days doth depend'. One of those fateful consequences follows immediately as Tybalt returns and is killed by Romeo.

In Zeffirelli's film, the fight is staged as a lengthy savage brawl, and there is a similar vicious struggle in Baz Luhrmann's film. In contrast, some stage productions have presented it as a formal sword-fencing duel. How a particular production stages the fight reveals the director's assumptions about the society and the characters in the play. Both Zeffirelli and Luhrmann use the fight to expose the viciousness that lies behind glamorous outward appearances in Verona. However the fight is staged, a further fateful consequence instantly threatens. Benvolio spells it out: the Prince will sentence Romeo to death. As he runs off to evade arrest, Romeo sees himself as the helpless victim of the mockery of mere chance:

> O, I am fortune's fool.　　　　　　　　　　　*(line 127)*

His perception of the cause of his anguish is immediately challenged. As the crowd gathers around Tybalt's body, Lady Capulet's reaction suggests that the venomous feud, rather than fortune, is responsible for Romeo's misery. She rejects Benvolio's explanation of the killings, accusing him of lying because he is a Montague. She twice calls for Romeo's death, and her demand to the Prince chillingly displays the hatred of the two families:

> For blood of ours, shed blood of Montague. *(line 140)*

Productions often suggest an additional cause of Lady Capulet's impassioned outburst. They show, in the 'party scene' (Act 1 Scene 5), an intimate, even sexual relationship between her and Tybalt. Shakespeare gives no explicit indication of that relationship, but on stage it can be convincing. As she now mourns over Tybalt's body, her language and actions can suggest that her relationship with Tybalt was something more than that of aunt to nephew. The Prince rejects both Lady Capulet's demand for death, and Montague's plea that his son should not be punished. Deaf to the 'pleading and excuses' of both families, the Prince banishes Romeo from Verona on pain of death:

> Let Romeo hence in haste,
> Else, when he is found, that hour is his last. *(lines 185–6)*

Act 3 Scene 2

Shakespeare immediately switches the scene from the bloodstained street to Juliet's bedroom. The dramatic juxtaposition is both striking and poignant. Juliet is unaware of the murderous events of the day and of Romeo's banishment. Filled with love for Romeo, she longs for the night to come. Her language is full of commands: 'Gallop apace', 'Spread thy close curtain', 'Come' (repeated six times), 'Hood', 'Give me my Romeo'. The sense of haste and speed created by the lines conveys the intensity of her feelings. Critics refer to her soliloquy as an *epithalamium*: a wedding song or poem in praise of the bride or groom. It was a popular genre in the sixteenth century, but Juliet's soliloquy is remarkable for its sexual content. Erotic meaning is both explicit ('amorous rites', etc.) and implicit ('die' was Elizabethan slang for sexual orgasm). Shakespeare makes it even more remarkable by having such physical longing spoken by a 13-year-old female character.

Juliet's soliloquy, for all its eager joy in the expectatio[n] contains ominous reminders of the gathering tragedy. [If] Phaeton were driving the chariot of the sun so that night [...] quickly. But in Greek mythology, Phaeton (son of Phoeb[us the sun] god) drove so recklessly that he was killed. Such an image [of] youthful rashness bodes ill for the lovers. So too does Juliet's imagining of her own death, with Romeo seemingly dismembered, cut out in little stars in the night sky. These inauspicious conceits become, for Juliet, menacingly real when the Nurse brings news of a death:

> We are undone, lady, we are undone.
> Alack the day, he's gone, he's killed, he's dead!   *(lines 38–9)*

Juliet mistakes the Nurse's mourning for Tybalt, thinking it is Romeo who is dead. Her grief is evident, but one aspect of it can create problems for a modern audience. Today, actors and audiences look for realism in outpourings of feeling. They value honesty of emotions. But Shakespeare's audiences expected and appreciated wordplay and punning, even in tragic episodes. So when Juliet and the Nurse, over eight lines (45–52), play obsessively with the vowel sound of 'I' ('ay', 'eye'), Elizabethan audiences responded with enthusiasm. But to modern ears, the 14 repetitions of the vowel sound make the lines seem artificial and contrived. They are often cut in performance.

At last Juliet learns the truth: Tybalt is dead and Romeo banished. Once again, her language takes a form that appealed to Elizabethan audiences but can seem contrived today. She accuses Romeo of seeming beautiful but acting vilely. In a long list of oxymorons ('beautiful tyrant', 'damned saint' and so on, see pages 7 and 74) she laments that a pleasing outward appearance can hide an evil reality: 'O that deceit should dwell in such a gorgeous palace!' Her words express the theme of the difference between appearance and reality (which is central to every one of Shakespeare's plays). But when the Nurse wishes shame on Romeo, Juliet rebukes her, and praises him extravagantly:

> Upon his brow shame is ashamed to sit;
> For 'tis a throne where honour may be crowned
> Sole monarch of the universal earth.   *(lines 92–4)*

throughout the entire scene, Juliet's moods swing violently. In this final episode, she tries to gain comfort from the fact that Romeo is alive, but is then devastated by the thought of his banishment. She threatens to kill herself, but is cheered by the Nurse's promise to find Romeo and send him to her bedchamber that night. The language of her final couplet reflects similarly wide contrasts. Its first line uses the formality of traditional tales of romantic chivalry. The simplicity of its second line echoes both the passion and the sense of approaching death of her opening speech in the scene:

> O find him! Give this ring to my true knight,
> And bid him come to take his last farewell.   *(lines 142–3)*

Act 3 Scene 3

Juliet has just described Romeo as her 'true knight'. Now, hiding in Friar Lawrence's cell, he appears to the Friar as a 'fearful man'. The descriptions contrast violently, but Romeo quickly shows that he shares the same emotional desolation as Juliet at hearing of his banishment. The thought appals him. His life lies only within Verona. Banishment is equivalent to death. Friar Lawrence rebukes him, claiming that the Prince has been merciful, because the law of Verona calls for death for death: Romeo's for Tybalt's.

Romeo will not be comforted. In lines which echo Juliet's wordplay in the previous scene, he laments that banishment means he can no longer be with Juliet. Once again, the language reveals differences between Shakespeare's own audiences and today's. Elizabethans enjoyed the comparisons: every cat, dog and little mouse may look on her; flies may even kiss her, but Romeo may not. Modern audiences can find the comparisons bizarre, and the punning artificial ('Flies may do this, but I from this must fly').

Perhaps Shakespeare had other reasons for these strange comparisons apart from their aural and imaginative appeal for his audiences. He may have written them to suggest Romeo's immaturity. Alternatively, he may have intended the triviality of the comparisons to suggest the depth of Romeo's feelings: even the tiniest thing assumes overwhelming importance in grief. The very personal agony Romeo experiences is embodied in his rebuke to the Friar, who, he believes, being sworn to celibacy, knows nothing of the sufferings of a young person in love:

Thou canst not speak of that thou dost not feel.   *(line 64)*

Romeo, bewailing all that has happened, falls weeping to the ground. The Friar, fearing that the Nurse's knocking at the door signals the arrival of officers to arrest Romeo, begs him to stand. Romeo refuses, but later obeys the Nurse's command (itself full of sexual innuendo): 'Stand up, stand up, stand, and you be a man'. The news of Juliet's sorrow provokes Romeo to an outburst against his name which so distresses her. His words eerily echo Juliet's 'What's in a name?' as he attempts to stab himself, wishing to cut out his name from his body. The Nurse snatches the dagger away and the Friar condemns his suicide attempt as lacking manliness, love and intelligence, because it would slay Juliet too.

The Friar then sets out to cheer Romeo's spirits, reminding him of his good fortune: Juliet lives, his deadly enemy Tybalt is dead, and he is only exiled not condemned to death. The Friar then proposes a plan. Romeo may spend the night with Juliet, then leave early in the morning for Mantua, from where he will eventually be recalled to live happily with her in Verona. In some productions the Friar obviously makes up his plan, little by little, on the spur of the moment, leaving the audience in no doubt that he has no idea about how he might effect the reconciliations whilst Romeo is in exile. But his plan impresses the Nurse ('O, what learning is!') and she sets out to prepare Juliet for Romeo's arrival. Romeo, too, sees hope and is assured by the Friar's promise to send news to him in Mantua. He leaves, expressing the infinity of his desire for his longed-for wedding night with Juliet:

a joy past joy calls out on me   *(line 173)*

Act 3 Scene 4

Shakespeare fills this short scene with dramatic irony (where the audience knows something a character does not). The audience has just seen Romeo preparing to spend the night with Juliet. They know that she is eagerly awaiting him in her bedroom. But Capulet has no knowledge of this, and he now plans to marry his daughter to Paris, kinsman to the Prince. Capulet is confident that Juliet will obey his wishes: 'I think she will be ruled in all respects by me'. That assumption of the supremacy of a father's authority would be shared by most members of Shakespeare's audience. Elizabethan England may have had a female as its monarch but, like Verona, it was a patriarchal society.

The dramatic irony tightens the tension of the drama by making conflict inevitable: what will happen when Juliet learns of her father's wish to marry her to Paris? Shakespeare increases the suspense through his handling of time in the scene. Its 35 lines contain well over 30 'time' words ('late', 'tonight', 'hour', 'tomorrow' and so on). The cumulative effect is to create the impression of time running ever faster towards inevitable disaster. The sense of events gathering momentum towards that tragedy is confirmed in the final speech as Capulet instructs his wife to tell Juliet she is to be married to Paris in three days' time. His final words on the lateness of the hour reveal that at this very moment Romeo and Juliet are in each other's arms and have physically consummated their secret marriage.

Act 3 Scene 5

Shakespeare's skill in creating dramatic juxtapositions is evident as the scene switches to Juliet's bedroom. Capulet's 'Good night' that ends Scene 4 is followed immediately by Juliet's protest as she tries to persuade Romeo not to go: 'Wilt thou be gone? It is not yet near day'. To heighten the contrast with Capulet's wedding plans for his daughter, many modern productions make it plain that Romeo and Juliet have spent a passionate night together.

Such contrasts foreshadow the conflicts that lie ahead, but at the scene's opening the conflict takes the form of an emotional struggle between the two lovers. Romeo feels he must leave, Juliet wants him to stay. Their expressively lyrical language as they dispute whether the nightingale or the lark has sung (the bird of night or day) cannot disguise the danger for Romeo if he is discovered:

> Night's candles are burnt out, and jocund day
> Stands tiptoe on the misty mountain tops.
> I must be gone and live, or stay and die.　　　　*(lines 9–11)*

Juliet momentarily prevails, and Romeo agrees to stay and face the consequence joyfully: 'Come, death, and welcome!' But his words alert Juliet to the dangerous reality of their situation and she orders him away. The Nurse's news that Lady Capulet is coming adds urgency to the lovers' parting. Their language becomes increasingly apprehensive and doom-laden. Their final words to each other are full of sombre foreboding:

JULIET   Methinks I see thee now, thou art so low,
         As one dead in the bottom of a tomb.
         Either my eyesight fails, or thou look'st pale.
ROMEO   And trust me, love, in my eye so do you:
         Dry sorrow drinks our blood. Adieu, adieu!   (lines 55–9)

Juliet weeps for the departed Romeo, but her mother mistakes her tears as grief for Tybalt's death. Juliet's replies to her mother are filled with double meaning. She has Romeo and love in mind, but Lady Capulet is thinking of Tybalt and revenge. For the audience, the mother–daughter exchanges are charged with dramatic irony as they see and hear Lady Capulet constantly deceived by Juliet's words. When Lady Capulet vows to have Romeo poisoned, Juliet's response expresses sexual desire for him, but her mother hears only confirmation of her own murderous intent.

But Lady Capulet's 'joyful tidings' provoke Juliet to speak plainly and directly. Hearing that her father plans to have her married to Paris, she flatly refuses. The news is so distressing that she again bursts into tears, which her father, now entering, also mistakes as sorrow for the dead Tybalt. Capulet seems to comfort Juliet, using an elaborate image of sea, ship and wind as metaphors for her eyes, body and sighs. Any good humour he might show quickly evaporates on learning that Juliet defies his wish that she marry Paris. Her riddling reply infuriates him, and he flies into a towering rage.

Juliet now endures a terrifying tongue-lashing from her father. Like many other fathers in Shakespeare's plays, Capulet attempts to dominate his daughter, and wishes her to obey his commands without question. He rebukes her, threatens to drag her on a hurdle to church, calls her insulting names, demands she obey him, comes close to physically assaulting her ('My fingers itch'), and threatens to disown her and throw her out of his house unless she marries Paris. His wife's and the Nurse's protests only infuriate him further. In words that echo the feelings of at least some members of Shakespeare's audience, Capulet makes clear that he regards Juliet as his possession, to be disposed of as he thinks fit, with the direst consequences if she disobeys:

And you be mine, I'll give you to my friend;
And you be not, hang, beg, starve, die in the streets

(lines 191–2)

Capulet storms out, swearing he will keep his word. Juliet, distraught, appeals to her mother to delay the marriage, or to see her dead in the Capulet tomb. But Lady Capulet refuses to help: 'Do as thou wilt, for I have done with thee'. Her refusal offers the opportunity for different interpretations of her character, for example whether she is afraid of her husband, or shares his impatience for his daughter, or is coldly indifferent to Juliet. But whatever her motivation, the dramatic effect is to isolate Juliet. That sense of isolation is made even more acute when Juliet appeals to the Nurse for comfort. The 'comfort' the Nurse provides is a further betrayal: she advises Juliet to marry Paris. Feeling she now can expect no help at home, Juliet sends the Nurse away, vowing never to trust her again. Significantly, the Act ends with Juliet quite alone. She resolves to seek the help of Friar Lawrence, but in a chilling final line expresses her resolve to kill herself if she cannot be reunited with Romeo:

If all else fail, myself have power to die.   *(line 242)*

Act 3: Critical review

Act 3 intensifies the sense of events gathering speed towards disaster. With the death of Mercutio, tragedy becomes inevitable. Romeo revenges Mercutio's death by killing Tybalt and, in consequence, is banished from Verona. Capulet orders Juliet to marry Paris, and her refusal provokes him to violent rage and leads to her abandonment by both her mother and her Nurse.

The Act also provides additional insight into character. Some critics claim that Juliet's violently changing moods, her defiance of her father, and her determination to take her own life if all else fails show evidence of her growing maturity. In contrast, Romeo's tearful behaviour in Friar Lawrence's cell suggests the immaturity that he has yet to overcome. The Friar is seen even more in the role of substitute father to Romeo. Capulet, shedding the geniality he displayed earlier in the play, explodes with rage at Juliet's disobedience. His tyrannical behaviour exposes the oppressive patriarchy that holds sway in Verona.

Mercutio's death raises a question that has long perplexed critics: why should Shakespeare kill off such a fascinating character so early in the play? All kinds of reasons suggest that Shakespeare was considering the dramatic effects of Mercutio's death:

- Mercutio had fulfilled his function in the plot.
- Shakespeare realised that Mercutio was unbalancing the play, attracting too much of the audience's interest and sympathy.
- He wished to focus the drama solely on the plight of the two young lovers.
- Mercutio's death adds to Romeo's anguish and despair.
- It sets the revenge aspect of the tragedy in motion.
- It is appropriate to the genre of tragedy in which good characters die needlessly, often as a result of accident.
- Mercutio's death, and the death of Tybalt that follows, intensifies the feud between the Montagues and Capulets.
- It links the 'private' and 'public' aspects of the play: Romeo, though deeply in love, is forced to accept the honour code of Verona's feuding society, and seek revenge. His 'public' action has dire consequences for his 'private' world: his love for Juliet.

Act 4 Scene 1

'On Thursday, sir? the time is very short.' The scene begins with Friar Lawrence's anxious response to what Paris has just told him. Paris now gives reasons for the haste in fixing the wedding day. Capulet wishes to have Juliet married very soon, because he believes a speedy marriage will stop her grieving for Tybalt. Once again, the audience is in possession of knowledge not shared by a character. They know that Paris, like Capulet, mistakenly believes that Juliet's sorrow is for Tybalt. The audience also shares Friar Lawrence's secret: he has married Romeo and Juliet. That knowledge adds dramatic irony to his replies to Paris because the audience realises that the Friar's unease about the proposed hasty marriage has its roots in reasons of which Paris is unaware. This dramatic situation, in which one character knows something another does not, is often referred to as 'discrepant awareness'.

The same discrepant awareness characterises Juliet's exchanges with Paris. It charges her responses with double meaning as she deflects each of his statements (just as she had done in her replies to her mother in the preceding scene). The audience knows that she always means more than Paris understands, but he leaves certain that he will marry Juliet on Thursday. The prospect appals her. She appeals to Friar Lawrence for help, twice threatening to kill herself if she is forced to marry Paris. At this point the audience and the two onstage characters are in a condition of equal awareness, but Shakespeare now raises the question of the Friar's motivation. The audience will be invited, in all that follows, to speculate about the motives that lie behind Friar Lawrence's terrifying plan that he proposes as the solution to Juliet's problems. As with all such questions of motivation, Shakespeare provides ample opportunities for a wide range of different interpretations.

Friar Lawrence sees hope in Juliet's unflinching willingness to kill herself, or to endure all kinds of terrifying and gruesome hazards rather than marry Paris. His plan is truly desperate. She must agree to marry Paris, but drink a potion which will make her seem dead. She will be placed in the Capulet vault, from where Romeo, recalled from Mantua by the Friar, will rescue her. Juliet instantly accepts the plan, and demands the potion: 'Give me, give me! O tell me not of fear'. In this scene, Shakespeare continues his dramatic development of Juliet's character. The 13-year-old girl displays a maturity and fearlessness that make her seem entirely different from how she appeared at the beginning of the play.

Act 4 Scene 2

Capulet is preparing for a grand wedding feast. He seems to have forgotten his earlier intention to have 'no great ado' as he orders 'twenty cunning cooks'. The brief exchange with the Servingman is another episode in which Shakespeare enables productions to create the bustling 'below stairs' life of the Capulet household. It can also yield insight into relationships between masters and servants in Verona. Here, the Servingman's banter suggests that the relationship is easy and informal. The opening also offers another brief opportunity (as in the celebrations of Act 1 Scene 5) for Capulet to show a genial aspect of his character.

The actor playing Capulet has a wide range of choice in how he speaks to Juliet ('How now, my headstrong, where have you been gadding?') and responds to her plea for forgiveness. He can be cold and stern, or can show warmth as he greets and listens to his daughter. But it is significant that his first words after Juliet's submission are an order to send for Paris and to shift the wedding date to the next morning. That precipitate action may suggest much about Capulet's self-centredness, and an actor who wishes to portray him very unsympathetically can legitimately choose to speak only two words directly to Juliet: 'stand up'. Crucially for the action, the hasty rearrangement of the wedding puts extra pressure on Juliet. She had expected a longer period of time before putting the Friar's dangerous plan into action.

Once again, Shakespeare uses the technique of 'discrepant awareness' to inject irony (see page 36). Capulet, not knowing of the Friar's plan to deceive him, praises 'this reverend holy Friar', declaring 'All our whole city is much bound to him'. Only Juliet and the audience know just how Friar Lawrence is really binding Verona, using a plot to deceive the city. Capulet brusquely overrules his wife, and insists again that the wedding take place the next day. Confident that all things are now as he wishes, Capulet declares he will take charge. He will make the wedding preparations himself, and will tell Paris to be ready to marry tomorrow. The audience is fully aware of the unconscious irony in Capulet's final words. His joy is misplaced, and his perception is mistaken:

My heart is wondrous light,
Since this same wayward girl is so reclaimed.   *(lines 45–6)*

Act 4 Scene 3

Shakespeare continues to deepen the irony as he now presents the
'reclaimed' Juliet in her bedroom. Everything she says to the Nurse
and her mother is charged with double meaning. They, like Capulet,
believe Juliet to be penitent, and willing to be married to Paris in the
morning. But the audience knows that her need for orisons (prayers),
and her 'state tomorrow' are quite different from what the Nurse and
her mother understand them to be. They think she is preparing for
marriage; Juliet and the audience know she is preparing for a state
that resembles death.

Lady Capulet and the Nurse leave, and Juliet fights her fears as she
tries to pluck up courage to drink the 'poison' that the Friar has given
her. She almost calls back the Nurse for comfort, but determines to
face her crisis alone. If the potion does not work, she resolves to kill
herself with her dagger. Her soliloquy is an outstanding example of
how Shakespeare gives the audience access to the inmost thoughts
and feelings of a character. It prefigures the soliloquies of Hamlet and
other tragic characters that Shakespeare would write five to ten years
after *Romeo and Juliet*.

Juliet's mind moves uneasily from one fearful thought to the next.
She wonders if the Friar intends to trick her by supplying a real
poison. Her death would conveniently rid him of the dishonour of
marrying her to Paris, knowing he has already married her to Romeo.
But as soon as she assures herself that the Friar is honest, her
imagination flits to the terrors of the tomb. What if she wakes before
Romeo arrives to rescue her? She imagines a horrible, stifling death,
or the madness she would be driven into by the ghastly sights, sounds
and smells that would surround her. Will her agony drive her to pluck
the dead Tybalt from his shroud, and dash out her own brains with an
ancestor's bone?

As her imagination races, and one dreadful fantasy gives way to
another, Juliet thinks she sees the ghost of Tybalt hunting down
Romeo. She cries out for him to stop. This effort to save Romeo restores
her courage. She calls to him three times, then drinks the potion. On
the Elizabethan stage it seems probable that Juliet would have fallen

back on her bed, which was concealed behind a curtain over the central entrance at the back of the stage. As will become clear, such a staging resolves the problem of how to play the two following scenes.

Act 4 Scenes 4 and 5

Scene 4 provides another glimpse of life in Capulet's household. It is early morning and the wedding preparations are well under way. Lady Capulet and the Nurse are about to get more food when Capulet bustles in, urging greater haste. Both women seem not to take him seriously. Their language allows for a range of stage interpretations. For example, the Nurse seems very familiar with her master, calling him 'cot-quean' (a man who does women's work). In some productions, Lady Capulet speaks bitterly, clearly suspecting her husband of being unfaithful. In reply, Capulet accuses her of jealousy. There is more banter between Capulet and the Servingmen, then Capulet sends the Nurse to wake Juliet.

Scene 5 flows on from Scene 4 without a break. On Shakespeare's stage, it is probable that the Nurse simply walked to the back of the stage and drew the curtain to reveal Juliet's bed. Modern productions nearly all follow the same principle, having the bed on stage, but ignored or partly concealed whilst Scene 4 is played. On film there is no 'location' problem because the camera can cut instantly to Juliet's bedroom, where she lies as if dead, the Friar's potion having taken effect. Whatever staging solution is decided, Scene 5 opens with the Nurse trying to wake Juliet:

> Why, lamb! why, lady! fie, you slug-a-bed!
> Why, love, I say! madam! sweet heart! why, bride!   *(lines 2–3)*

The Nurse's language is typically full of exclamations, colloquialisms and sexual jokes about Juliet's wedding night. But as all her attempts to rouse Juliet fail, the Nurse suddenly concludes that her young mistress is dead. Her cries bring Lady Capulet, who grieves for her only child: 'O me, O me, my child, my only life! / Revive, look up, or I will die with thee.' Capulet then enters and expresses his sorrow in a memorable image:

> Death lies on her like an untimely frost
> Upon the sweetest flower of all the field.   *(lines 28–9)*

On stage, the joyous sounds of the approaching wedding party contrast starkly with the scene of grief around Juliet's bed. Friar Lawrence, Paris and the musicians come crowding in, usually to freeze dramatically, the music dying away, as they grasp what is happening. The episode that follows, the 'mourning scene' of lines 35–64 and 84–90 has fiercely divided critics. Some dismiss the episode, judging the language as artificial and insincere. They argue that Shakespeare is writing a parody here, mocking such ceremonious mourning. For example, Frank Kermode claims that 'With extraordinary boldness Shakespeare makes these sorrows absurd', and condemns the Nurse's language in particular: 'It is as if the Nurse had strayed in from a production by Bottom'.

Some stage directors appear to share this stern critical judgement and cut the episode drastically in performance. But those critics who argue for the sincerity of feeling that underpins the 'mourning lines' of each character draw support from two sources. First, in some stagings the episode can be extraordinarily effective, conveying both the drama and the emotional intensity of the lines. Second, although the language is formal and excessively heightened, it is judged entirely appropriate to the genre within which Shakespeare was working. There are many examples elsewhere in the literature and drama of the time that use similar language styles to express grief. Shakespeare's Elizabethan audiences would have valued those very features of the language which some modern critics condemn as blatantly artificial.

Yet another critical interpretation of these 'mourning lines' argues that Shakespeare intended them to be spoken simultaneously, not heard in their own right. However, it is open to each reader or spectator of the play to make up their own mind on these issues. That judgement may be affected in part by Friar Lawrence's speech in which he rebukes the mourners. He urges them to cease sorrowing because Juliet is now in heaven. But the Friar (and the audience) knows what the grieving mourners do not: Juliet is alive. That realisation adds both irony and poignancy to Capulet's closing speech in which he uses a long series of antitheses to lament the change from festival to funeral, from joy to sorrow:

> All things that we ordainèd festival,
> Turn from their office to black funeral:
> Our instruments to melancholy bells,

Our wedding cheer to a sad burial feast;
Our solemn hymns to sullen dirges change;
Our bridal flowers serve for a buried corse;
And all things change them to the contrary.   *(lines 84–90)*

With the departure of the mourners, only the musicians are left on stage, and the mood changes to one of bathos (anti-climax). Peter, the Nurse's servant, enters and variously insults, threatens and mocks the musicians. They do not seem to enjoy his humour: 'What a pestilent knave', 'Hang him'. The episode has puzzled critics because of its seeming triviality. Some argue that Shakespeare did not write it, but that it was inserted by Thomas Nashe, whose style it resembles. Others argue it was written as a 'turn' for Will Kemp, a famous comic in Shakespeare's acting company, who played Peter. Yet others argue that the episode is typically Shakespearean, first in providing dramatic contrast to the grieving of the upper-class characters, and second because it reminds the audience that, even when confronted by terrible tragedy, the trivialities of ordinary life go on: Peter cracks poor jokes and the musicians simply hope for a tip and a free meal. The episode is often cut in modern productions.

Act 4: Critical review

Throughout Act 4, Shakespeare directs the dramatic focus unceasingly upon Juliet and her plight. Romeo is kept offstage, the Nurse is no longer Juliet's trusted confidante. Juliet must face the consequences of her dangerous action quite alone, and she faces the challenge with extraordinary maturity and bravery. In Scene 1 she agrees to the Friar's hazardous plan. In Scene 2 her pretended submission to her father prompts him to bring forward the wedding to the very next day, thus intensifying the pressure she is under. In Scene 3 she deceives her Nurse and mother, leaving them unaware of her true intention to seemingly kill herself. Her soliloquy takes the audience into the agony of her innermost thoughts and feelings.

Even in 'death' Juliet's presence dominates the final scene as her parents, the Nurse and Paris grieve over her body. In the eighteenth century, the Act ended with a magnificent funeral procession as the Capulets bore their daughter's body to the Capulet tomb. That scene is rarely, if ever, played today. But even when the concluding downbeat and comic episode with the musicians is performed, the final impression of Act 4 is to prepare the audience for Act 5: what will be Romeo's response to the news of the death of Juliet?

The irony that characterises each scene is created through Shakespeare's constant use of 'discrepant awareness' (in which a character is unaware of the true meaning of what another character says). The audience knows that Paris does not understand the real significance of what Juliet says to him. Similarly, Capulet believes that she agrees to marry Paris, and the Nurse and Lady Capulet mistake her desire to be left alone the night before the marriage. The irony is deepened in the 'grieving' episode. The audience knows that all the mourners are misled by appearances, and that the Friar's consoling words conceal his plan to deceive the Capulets.

The Act also provides brief glimpses of the 'below stairs' bustle of the Capulet household. The appearances of low-status servants and musicians are reminders that alongside the unfolding tragedy everyday life goes on. Such moments contrast dramatically with the sense of death that pervades the Act. To everyone except Friar Lawrence, it really does seem that Death has taken Juliet as his bride.

Act 5 Scene 1

The scene shifts to Mantua, and finds Romeo joyfully describing a strange dream he has had. In the real world, Mantua is 25 miles from Verona, but on stage the scene change must be effected quickly and convincingly. On the bare Elizabethan stage there were no elaborate sets to indicate the change of location. Shakespeare relied on language, the actor's presence, and the power of his audience's imagination. On modern stages the resources of lighting and technology can speedily effect the change, for example by 'flying in' a piece of scenery. On film, the change of location is even more easily accomplished in an instantaneous 'cut'. For example, Baz Luhrmann's film sets the scene in a run-down trailer park in the desert.

Romeo's description of his dream is brief but ominous. He dreamed that Juliet found him dead, but revived him with kisses. In Scene 3 his dream will acquire cruel dramatic irony when Juliet kisses his dead lips in an attempt to kill herself. That irony is immediately foreshadowed as Balthasar brings dreadful news from Verona: Juliet is dead. Romeo's response is a defiant challenge against the fates that he feels are controlling his life: 'then I defy you, stars!' His challenge echoes the unease he expressed at the end of Act 1 Scene 4 just before he went to Capulet's feast: 'my mind misgives / Some consequence yet hanging in the stars'.

Dismissing Balthasar to hire horses for their return to Verona, Romeo resolves to kill himself that night in the tomb with Juliet. But how? The apothecary who sells poison comes into his mind. Romeo's detailed and sinister description of the Apothecary and his shop is an example of Shakespeare's imagination being fired by his reading and experience. Brooke's long poem (the source of *Romeo and Juliet*, see page 55) has only the very briefest description, but in Elizabethan London there were such shops displaying the curious items that Romeo lists. For some unknown reason, Shakespeare adds that the Apothecary's shop is shut because it is a holiday in Mantua. That detail can in turn help to fire the imagination of directors of the play. For example, in a production for the Royal Shakespeare Company, Michael Bogdanov used Romeo's brief comment to create a carnival scene, with revellers carrying giant papier-mache heads of contemporary politicians.

The penniless Apothecary sells poison to Romeo, even though he knows the penalty for doing so is death. The 40 ducats that Romeo pays was a very large amount of money in Shakespeare's time. Its size may indicate the high value Romeo puts on death: he willingly pays for a poison that will enable him to die alongside Juliet. But some critics (following Karl Marx's comments on the episode) see further significance in the 40 ducats. They argue that because a ducat is a gold coin, Shakespeare seizes the opportunity to comment critically on the poisonous power of money in Elizabethan England. They highlight Romeo's lines as he hands over the coins:

> There is thy gold, worse poison to men's souls,
> Doing more murder in this loathsome world,
> Than these poor compounds that thou mayst not sell.
> I sell thee poison, thou hast sold me none.   *(lines 80–3)*

Such interpretations raise important questions about the value of extracting a quotation to support a particular point of view. What is certain is that Shakespeare's personal views on any matter are unknown. His plays have been selectively used to support virtually every possible and starkly opposing view of any matter. Here, Romeo is criticising the poisonous power of money, and it is advisable to base interpretation on the evidence within the play itself. For example, it might be argued that the corrosive feud between the Montagues and Capulets has its origins in a quarrel over some matter of wealth (but that, too, is only a speculation). But whatever the motivation lying behind Romeo's condemnation, his emotions and thoughts are focused only on Juliet. He leaves for Verona and Juliet's tomb, determined to drink the potion there, and die.

Act 5 Scene 2

This brief scene reveals why Romeo, exiled in Mantua, has heard nothing from Friar Lawrence. The Friar had written a letter explaining his plot, assuring Romeo that Juliet is not really dead, and calling him back to take her from the tomb. He entrusted the letter to his fellow Franciscan, Friar John. But John now tells how an unlucky mischance prevented him delivering the letter. He called first upon another Franciscan friar, who he hoped would accompany him to Mantua. He found him visiting the sick. Disaster struck. The 'searchers' called at the house where the infected lived and discovered the two friars there.

The 'searchers' were health officers of the city. They were appointed to prevent the spread of disease by examining dead bodies

to establish the cause of death. The searchers though[']
raged in the house, and so refused the two Francisc[']
leave or travel ('sealed up the doors'). This was c[']
English cities at the time Shakespeare wrote the play [.]
searchers did would seem familiar and justified to his audi[.]

Friar Lawrence is anguished by this chance accident: 'Unha[p,]
fortune!' He sends Friar John for a crowbar, and determines to break
into Capulet's monument to be with Juliet when she wakes. His final
line expresses the macabre situation in which Juliet is trapped:

> Poor living corse, closed in a dead man's tomb!   *(line 30)*

Act 5 Scene 3

Friar Lawrence's final line in the previous scene prepares the audience
for the setting of the final scene: a churchyard within which is the
monument of the Capulets. The scene poses particular problems of
staging because the action takes place both outside and inside the
tomb. On Shakespeare's own stage, Juliet probably lay on a bier
concealed behind a curtain at the back of the stage. In the nineteenth
century all kinds of very elaborate tomb settings and scenery were
constructed, but since the twentieth century sets have become much
less realistic.

In stage productions today, sets for the scene tend to be fairly
simple. As in Shakespeare's time, they rely on the audience's
imaginative response to language to create location and atmosphere.
Shakespeare provides help in abundance. The scene's first episode, in
which Paris visits the tomb to lay flowers and to mourn, is rich in
words and phrases which create the location and atmosphere of a
churchyard at night: 'torch', 'yew trees', 'hollow ground', 'churchyard',
'graves' and so on.

Paris orders his Page to keep watch and whistle to warn of
intruders. He then strews flowers and mourns, promising to repeat
the ritual each night. Hearing his Page's whistle, Paris conceals
himself to discover who disturbs his private funeral rites. It is Romeo
and Balthasar. Romeo is determined to force open the tomb and die
alongside Juliet, but he lies to Balthasar, telling him that he only
wishes to gaze on Juliet and to recover a ring from her finger. In sharp
contrast to Paris' formal rhymes, Romeo uses extravagantly hyperbolic
blank verse to dismiss Balthasar on pain of death:

By heaven, I will tear thee joint by joint,
And strew this hungry churchyard with thy limbs.
The time and my intents are savage-wild,
More fierce and more inexorable far
Than empty tigers or the roaring sea.   *(lines 35–9)*

Balthasar, in an aside, resolves to stay and watch. His decision creates another staging problem: there are now three 'watchers' to be concealed (Paris, his Page, Balthasar). That practical problem reveals two major conventions of Shakespeare's own theatre: non-realistic staging, and the demand on the audience's imagination. A modern way of expressing those conventions might be 'the willingness of the audience to suspend its disbelief'. That willingness is usually achieved with the audience accepting that the three 'watchers' can 'hide' in non-realistic ways.

Romeo begins to force entry into the tomb. Paris, fearing Romeo's intention is to desecrate the dead bodies inside, steps forward to challenge him. Romeo does not recognise Paris and orders him away. But Paris persists, determined to arrest Romeo. They fight, and Paris is mortally wounded. With his dying breath, he begs to be laid beside Juliet. At last, Romeo recognises who he has slain and struggles desperately to recall why he knows that Paris should have married Juliet. His confusion (Was he told it? Did he dream it? Is he mad?) yields to a desire for forgiveness. His description of the dead Paris and himself might well stand for other characters afflicted by unhappy mischance and accident, Mercutio, Tybalt and Juliet:

O give me thy hand,
One writ with me in sour misfortune's book!   *(lines 81–2)*

The scene moves 'inside' the tomb as Romeo lays Paris near to Juliet. The move is easily accomplished in most modern stagings because Juliet's bier is usually centre stage and the preceding action occurs close to it. On film the change of location can be dazzling. Baz Luhrmann showed Juliet lying in magnificent state in a cathedral, bathed in the light of thousands of candles. Luhrmann, like many directors, wishes quite literally to highlight Romeo's image of Juliet's beauty making the vault 'a feasting presence full of light' (a 'feasting presence' was a magnificent banqueting room in a royal palace).

Romeo's final soliloquy intensifies that image as he admires Juliet's beauty and reflects that death has not succeeded in tarnishing it in any way:

> Thou art not conquered, beauty's ensign yet
> Is crimson in thy lips and in thy cheeks,
> And Death's pale flag is not advancèd there.   *(lines 94–6)*

His words take on a terrible irony, because he speaks a truth he does not realise: Juliet is alive. But unaware that she lives, Romeo pursues his purpose of self-destruction. He begs Tybalt for forgiveness, then imagines that Death wants Juliet as a lover. To prevent that, he determines to stay perpetually with Juliet, joining her in death. His soliloquy echoes many of the previous images and concerns of the play: death, love, light in darkness, 'inauspicious stars'. His final image is addressed to the poison: 'bitter conduct', 'unsavoury guide'. It recalls a similar image at the end of Act 1 Scene 4, spoken just before he entered Capulet's house and first saw Juliet. Then, he appealed to God to guide his life's voyage. Now Romeo portrays life as a dangerous sea journey which ends wrecked on 'dashing rocks'. At his own journey's end he drinks the poison, kisses Juliet, and dies.

A number of modern productions have intensified the dramatic irony of Romeo's final moments. Throughout his final soliloquy he is unaware that Juliet is alive, but sometimes the audience see her showing signs of reviving before Romeo dies. The irony becomes even more agonisingly acute if Romeo, having swallowed the poison, sees Juliet returning to life. It can create a bitterly tragic atmosphere as Romeo realises the tragic waste of his life, and that his own mistaken action has cruelly snatched away the happiness he might have enjoyed with Juliet. Some critics dislike such staging, arguing that there is no evidence that Shakespeare wanted Romeo to be aware that Juliet is alive and so wrote the intensely eloquent speech intending it to be a triumphant affirmation of love. But the interpretation can create a powerful dramatic effect on stage.

Shakespeare now switches the action back to the churchyard where Friar Lawrence, arriving in haste, breathlessly asks Balthasar why a light burns in the Capulet monument. Balthasar explains that Romeo is inside, and fearfully refuses to accompany the Friar into the tomb.

Friar Lawrence is astonished that Romeo, whom he thought to be still in Mantua, is here in Verona. Entering the tomb, he discovers the bodies of Romeo and Paris. The episode places great demands on the actor playing Lawrence. His language is full of words and phrases that convey urgency and fear, and his many short sentences suggest that his mind leaps desperately from one anxious thought to the next. His plan has gone disastrously wrong, and he seems close to panic.

The pressure on Friar Lawrence increases as Juliet wakes and asks 'Where is my Romeo?' The Friar's response has led to his being condemned by many critics and spectators. He tries to take Juliet away, intending to hide her in a convent with 'a sisterhood of holy nuns', but then simply abandons her: 'I dare no longer stay'. Friar Lawrence's critics see his running away as a callous, self-centred action. But a different way of looking at it is to speculate that Shakespeare wished to increase further the sense of Juliet's isolation. Perhaps the playwright felt that it was more dramatically effective to remove the Friar so that Juliet must act her final scene entirely alone.

Shakespeare gives Juliet a much shorter 'death speech' than Romeo. The brevity can heighten the audience's impression of her courage. She resolutely refuses to leave the tomb, seeks for any last drops of poison, then kisses Romeo's lips in the hope of finding poison there. Hearing the Captain of the Watch approaching, she kills herself with Romeo's dagger:

> O happy dagger,
> This is thy sheath; there rust, and let me die.   (lines 169–70)

Some critics have objected to Juliet's word 'rust'. Dover Wilson thought it 'hideously unpoetic', and preferred the alternative 'rest'. Other critics find 'rust' appropriate because it suggests the decay that follows death. However, much more important is the finality and bravery of her action. She does not flinch from death but embraces it willingly, believing it will unite her for ever with Romeo. Juliet's action completes a memorable stage tableau (frozen picture). She and Romeo lie united in death, encircled by the dead bodies of Paris, Tybalt and long-dead Capulets.

In the nineteenth century, many productions ended the play with that striking stage picture of the two lovers, free at last from the cruel oppression of fortune and the feud. But Shakespeare has not yet completed his play. In a flurry of dramatic activity, as entrance follows entrance, all the remaining characters assemble at the tomb. Balthasar and Friar Lawrence are brought in under guard, and the Prince takes charge. The Capulets enter the tomb and are devastated by the sight. Montague arrives, reports his wife is dead, and he too enters the tomb and returns grieving.

The Prince promises to investigate, and to punish wrongdoers with death. At the Prince's command, Friar Lawrence, Balthasar and Paris' Page relate their stories (fearfully in some productions, as if expecting punishment). The style of their accounts is remarkably different from most of the language of the play. It is plain narrative, without wordplay or puns, and with very little imagery. Many productions severely reduce these speeches, or cut them entirely, together with the Prince's few lines recounting the contents of Romeo's letter. But most stagings give full weight to Montague and the Capulets grieving over their dead children, and then move to the Prince's commanding rebuke as he orders them to look on the deadly results of their quarrel:

> Where be these enemies? Capulet, Montague?
> See what a scourge is laid upon your hate,
> That heaven finds means to kill your joys with love!
>
> *(lines 291–3)*

Here, some productions crowd the stage with citizens of Verona in order to intensify the social relevance of the tragedy. The people's presence acknowledges that the deaths have been caused by the bitter enmity of the two families. Society must now witness the appalling consequences and hear how Montague and Capulet, the leaders of the two factions, might heal Verona's fractured community.

The closing moments of the tragedy were traditionally played to suggest that the death of the young lovers has a good consequence: it ends the feud. Capulet and Montague shake hands, make up their quarrel, and promise to set up golden statues of Romeo and Juliet. The Prince acknowledges the sorrow of the time, but sees peace ahead for Verona. But some recent productions, following contemporary preferences in literature and drama for enigmatic or unsettling endings, have not ended on a note of reconciliation and the promise of future harmony.

Such productions show clearly that the bitter feud will continue.

The prospect of future conflict is signified by the families' physical separation on stage, and their leaving in opposite directions. The apparently conciliatory words of Montague and Capulet are presented as a cynical public relations exercise in which 'spin' masks very real hostility and a desire to outbid each other in conspicuous display of gold. Such productions often emphasise that something more than a desire for justice lies behind the Prince's promise of punishment for those who have caused the tragedy. The effect is to suggest that the rottenness that lies at the heart of Verona's society remains festering and malign. The play's openness to such contrasting portrayals testifies to Shakespeare's playwriting skill. That skill enables each ending to be dramatically convincing, each in their different way justifying the couplet with which the Prince ends the play:

> For never was a story of more woe
> Than this of Juliet and her Romeo.   *(lines 309–10)*

Act 5: Critical review

Act 5 ends with a cruel irony. As Friar Lawrence hoped, the feud has apparently ended, but not in the way he intended. His plan envisaged that the marriage of Romeo and Juliet should end the strife that tears Verona apart. But it is their children's death that causes Montague and Capulet to shake hands.

The sense of tragedy is heightened by Paris' death. Like the death of Romeo and Juliet, his is another innocent young life needlessly destroyed. The sense of waste is palpable. The Prince's final words, promising pardon or punishment, raise the question of who or what is to blame. Act 5 suggests a number of causes of the tragedy:

- Romeo's challenge 'Then I defy you, stars!' suggests two major possible causes: fate and free will. It shows that Romeo chooses to bring about his own death (free will) in defiance of what any supernatural influence (fate) has decreed up to this moment.
- Scene 2 suggests the role of accident and chance in the tragedy. The failure of Friar John to deliver Friar Lawrence's letter is yet another 'accident' of fortune that makes disaster inevitable.
- The Prince's reproach to Capulet and Montague, 'See what a scourge is laid upon your hate', suggests that the tragedy has a social cause: the feud that has racked the city.

The effect upon the audience of this final Act will much depend on how it is performed. For example, they may feel strong agreement or disagreement with the production's presentation of Montague and Capulet's handshake: is the feud really ended? They might be angered by Friar Lawrence's abandonment of Juliet. But all productions hope that the audience will respond feelingly to the lovers' last moments, perhaps in the ways suggested by critic and director John Russell Brown:

> Wonder is likely to be its dominant response but it may also feel shocked, bruised, depleted, indignant, outraged, trapped, or bemused, implicated in some immediate and very personal way.

Contexts

The hugely enjoyable film *Shakespeare in Love* portrays a popular belief about the source of Shakespeare's creativity. It shows him suffering from 'writer's block', unable to put pen to paper, with no idea of how to write his next play. But all is resolved when he meets a beautiful young girl. His love for her sparks an overwhelming flow of creative energy – and he writes *Romeo and Juliet*!

It is an attractive idea, and the film presents it delightfully, but the truth of the matter is far more complex. Like every other writer, Shakespeare was influenced by many factors other than his own personal experience. The society of his time, its practices, beliefs and language in political and economic affairs, culture and religion, were the raw materials on which his imagination worked.

This chapter first identifies the three texts from which all later editions of *Romeo and Juliet* derive. It then discusses the contexts from which *Romeo and Juliet* emerged: the wide range of different influences which fostered the creativity of Shakespeare as he wrote the play. These contexts ensured that *Romeo and Juliet* is full of all kinds of reminders of everyday life and of the familiar knowledge, assumptions, beliefs and values of Elizabethan England.

What did Shakespeare write?

Sometime around 1594, William Shakespeare, rapidly becoming known as a successful playwright, wrote *Romeo and Juliet*. It was probably first performed in 1595. What was the play that Shakespeare wrote and his audiences heard? No one knows for certain because his original script has not survived, nor any handwritten amendments he might subsequently have made. So what is the origin of the text of the play you are studying? Most scholars today agree with the following account of how the text of today's editions was established.

The first published version of the play appeared in 1597 and is known as the First Quarto (a quarto page is about the same size as this page you are reading). Its title page described it as 'An excellent conceited tragedy of Romeo and Juliet', and boasted that it was already popular on stage. This First Quarto is usually regarded as an unreliable 'pirate' version, compiled from memory by two actors in order to cash in on the play's success on stage.

In 1599, another edition was published (the Second Quarto). Its title page read 'The most excellent and lamentable tragedy of Romeo and Juliet. Newly corrected, augmented and amended'. This Second Quarto is usually thought to be the response of Shakespeare's Acting Company to the pirate First Quarto published two years earlier. Many scholars regard it as the Company's 'official' account of the play, intended to establish the authentic version. They believe it is based on Shakespeare's original manuscript ('foul papers') or a copy of it. The Second Quarto is 800 lines longer than the First Quarto, and many of its words and phrases are different from those in the First Quarto (it also puzzlingly gives the same four lines to both Romeo and Friar Lawrence, see page 19).

Today, nearly all editions of the play are based on the Second Quarto, because it is thought to be closest to Shakespeare's intentions. But in preparing the play for publication, modern editors take close account of the First Quarto. They consider it especially valuable for its stage directions, which are far more detailed than those in the Second Quarto. Indeed, some scholars argue that because of its precise stage directions and its comparative brevity, the First Quarto is an acting version intended to be performed in 'the two hours' traffic' of the stage. Modern editors also take account of two other Quartos published in 1609 and 1622 (both based on the Second Quarto), and the version of the play in the First Folio of 1623 (a folio page is about two times larger than this page you are reading). The First Folio, containing 36 plays, was published in 1623, seven years after Shakespeare's death.

So, the text of *Romeo and Juliet* is not as stable as you might think. The edition of the play you are using will vary from other editions. That is because every edition is the result of an editor making a multitude of judgements as he or she looks at the various versions of the play published during or shortly after Shakespeare's lifetime. This is no reason for dismay, however, because these differences reflect what happens in performance: every production, on stage or film, cuts, adapts and amends the text to present its own unique version of *Romeo and Juliet*. And, as you will discover on page 99, for almost 100 years a very different version of the play was staged from what is usually seen today. This guide follows the New Cambridge edition of the play (also used in the Cambridge School Shakespeare edition) which, like all today's major editions, is based on the Second Quarto.

What did Shakespeare read?

Shakespeare's genius lay in his ability to transform what he read into gripping drama. This section is therefore about the influence of genre: the literary contexts of *Romeo and Juliet* in both elite and popular culture. It identifies the stories and dramatic conventions that fired Shakespeare's imagination as he wrote *Romeo and Juliet*.

The story of Romeo and Juliet was well known long before Shakespeare gave it dramatic life. It existed throughout much of Europe in numerous folk tales, myths and ballads which contained a similar storyline of lovers from opposing families who chose death rather than be parted. Various ingredients of this story of 'separation-romance' occurred in different versions: the wooing at a window, potions to fake death, a lover's night visit, and other incidents that appear in Shakespeare's play.

Many traditional versions of the story contained stock characters: meddlesome friars who concoct deceitful plans, a garrulous old nurse, an angry father and, of course, young lovers for whom the path of true love does not run smooth. Many in Shakespeare's audience would see Romeo as a love-melancholic, a popular stereotype in the literature of the time (but best known in a book published about 25 years later: Robert Burton's *The Anatomy of Melancholy*, 1621). In the play's first scene, Romeo's hiding away from family and friends and sorrowing over Rosaline resemble such a character's emotional instability and depression.

Was there any historical truth in the tales? Around 1290, two Italian families, the Montecchi and the Capelletti, became notorious for a feud in which they destroyed each other. The great Italian poet Dante used their story as a warning that society would destroy itself if such feuds went unchecked. But historically there is no record that the families had children called Romeo and Juliet, and whilst the Montecchi lived in Verona, the Capelletti lived in Cremona, 60 miles distant.

Shakespeare would have known such tales and ballads. They were part of the popular culture of his time, and they would have been in his mind as he wrote the play. But it is possible to identify three other very specific influences on Shakespeare from which he created *Romeo and Juliet*: a long poem by Arthur Brooke, the sonnet tradition, and the Elizabethans' appetite for tragedy on stage.

Arthur Brooke, *The Tragicall Historye of Romeus and Juliet*

Shakespeare read a version of the story in a long poem by Arthur Brooke, *The Tragicall Historye of Romeus and Juliet*, first published in 1562. Brooke himself had gone back to earlier versions of the tale. His poem was based on a French adaptation of an Italian story by Matteo Bandello, *Romeo e Giulietta*. It seems certain that Shakespeare had Brooke's poem in front of him as he wrote *Romeo and Juliet*, because the play follows Brooke's narrative sequence very closely, and contains many verbal echoes of the poem's language.

But Shakespeare transformed Brooke's dull and rambling poem into thrilling drama. He reordered events, for example by having the feud explode into violent action in the very first scene with Tybalt as chief troublemaker. In Brooke, the fight and Tybalt's entry are long delayed. Shakespeare telescopes events into four days, increasing the speed and dramatic tension of the action. In contrast, there is little pressure of events in Brooke, where the action stretches over at least nine months. Shakespeare's compression of time thus greatly heightens the emotional impact of the drama.

Shakespeare also created complex dramatic characters out of Brooke's stereotypes. Romeo, Juliet, the Nurse and Friar Lawrence acquire far greater personal and dramatic depth. In Shakespeare's poetic and dramatic imagination these characters are quite different from the stock figures of traditional folk tales. Shakespeare reduces Juliet's age from 16 (as she is in Brooke) to only 13. As pages 64–5 show, making her only 13 greatly affected audience reaction in Shakespeare's time. Mercutio is entirely Shakespeare's invention. His character, his function as mocking commentator on romantic love, and how the manner of his death causes Romeo to seek revenge are entirely absent from Brooke. Most significantly, Mercutio's language, like that of every other character, displays how far Shakespeare's verbal facility and emotional register soars above Brooke's pedestrian verse.

Using his skills as a playwright, Shakespeare gave a powerful dramatic structure to the story. The play's opening creates a telling impression of a community divided against itself, and the three appearances of Prince Escales provide a strong opening, centre and close to the drama. Other dramatic structurings include the significant contrasts and parallels of character. Benvolio's peace-making is set against Tybalt's aggression. Mercutio and the Nurse become major comic characters and share similar functions as confidantes of the lovers and mockers of romantic love. Mercutio's death becomes the motive for Romeo's revenge, with tragic consequences. Paris is made a rival suitor to Romeo and killed by him. Both men lie beside Juliet in death. Throughout, as the Commentary shows (pages 5–51), Shakespeare's stagecraft juxtaposes scenes to intensify dramatic effect.

Both Shakespeare's play and Brooke's poem show how extreme passion leads to disaster: 'violent delights have violent ends'. But the tone of the play is quite different from the poem, and it is open to an infinitely greater range of interpretation. It is always dangerous to speculate about Shakespeare's intentions, but it seems obvious the play does not share Brooke's moralistic assumptions about the tale he was telling. The play does not make clear whether Shakespeare endorses or condemns the young lovers' actions and disobedience. In sharpest contrast, in his introduction to the poem, Brooke reduces the Nurse to a drunken gossip and Friar Lawrence to a superstitious priest, and strongly condemns Romeo and Juliet, blaming them for bringing disaster on their own heads:

> a couple of unfortunate lovers, thralling themselves to unhonest desire, neglecting the authority and advice of parents and friends, conferring their principal counsels with drunken gossips and superstitious friars . . . for the attaining of their wished lust . . . abusing the honourable name of lawful marriage, to cloak the shame of stolen contracts, finally, by all means of unhonest life, hastening to most unhappy death

The sonnet tradition

Romeo and Juliet opens with a sonnet (the Prologue), and several other sonnets are spoken in the play (Lady Capulet's description of Paris, the lovers' first words to each other, Chorus at the end of Act 1). The influence of the sonnet tradition is evident throughout the language of the play in the extravagant imagery ('conceits'), wordplay, repetition, hyperbole and oxymorons (see pages 72–83). Shakespeare makes conscious acknowledgement to the source of the sonnet tradition when he has Mercutio exclaim:

> Now is he for the numbers that Petrarch flowed in. Laura to
> his lady was a kitchen wench (marry, she had a better love to
> berhyme her)   *(Act 2 Scene 4, lines 34–6)*

Mercutio laughs at Romeo, accusing him of being ready to write
verse ('numbers') to 'his lady' who makes Laura seem like 'a kitchen
wench'. What lies behind Mercutio's mockery? Who was Laura and
the man ('a better love') who wrote poems to her ('berhyme her')? The
answer to each question lies in what has become known as 'the sonnet
tradition'.

Well over two hundred years before Shakespeare was born, an
Italian poet living in Avignon in the South of France caught sight of a
woman who was to inspire some of the most famous love poetry of all
time. The poet was Francesco Petrarca, known as Petrarch (1304–74).
He called the woman Laura, but her real identity is not known.

Long after Laura's death, Petrarch collected together the poems he
had written about her. His *Rime* (or *Canzoniere*) enjoyed huge
popularity. It began a tradition in which the 14-line sonnet was used
by a man to declare unwavering devotion to a beautiful but cold and
disdainful lady. With great lyrical intensity, each sonnet told of the
poet's suffering as the unattainable woman cruelly and implacably
refused his advances. Sonnets expressed the poetry of frustration, of
unrequited love.

Although sonnets flourished in Italy and France, they were only
slowly taken up by English poets. For example, Geoffrey Chaucer
(1345–1400) included a translation of one of Petrarch's sonnets in his
Troilus and Criseyde, but it was only much later that Sir Thomas Wyatt
(1503–42) and the Earl of Surrey (1517–47) made the sonnet form
familiar to English readers. Wyatt translated many of Petrarch's
sonnets into English, and added a new 'anti-Petrarchan' theme: the
desire of the lover to break free of the love that enslaves him. Surrey
established the rhyme scheme that was to become known as the
'English' or 'Shakespearean' sonnet.

The poems of Wyatt and Surrey were published in 1557, but it was
not until the 1590s that sonnets became really popular. In 1591, Sir
Philip Sidney's sonnet sequence *Astrophil and Stella* was published. It
sparked off a brief but glitteringly intense and fruitful period, when
writing and reading sonnets became a vogue among the educated
classes. In 1586, Sidney had died aged only 31. He was fatally wounded

in a siege in the Low Countries (Holland), and a legend quickly grew
that turned him into a great hero. That legend contributed to the wildly
enthusiastic reception that greeted his sonnet sequence. It began not
just a fashion but a craze for sonnets which lasted for a decade.

Everyone who considered himself a poet (at that time nearly all
poetry was written by men) tried his hand at sonnets. It became the
most fashionable literary activity of all, and poets took an obsessive
delight in wordplay. Shakespeare joined in. Because of striking
similarities between his play and his sonnets it seems virtually certain
that he wrote many of his sonnets shortly before or at the same time
as he was writing *Romeo and Juliet*. Indeed, *Sonnet 29* seems almost
as if it could be spoken by Romeo in his anguish at his banishment
from Juliet. It begins:

> When in disgrace with Fortune and men's eyes,
> I all alone beweep my outcast state,
> And trouble deaf heaven with my bootless cries,
> And look upon myself and curse my fate   *(Sonnet 29, lines 1–4)*

The contemporary popularity of sonnets ensured that many people
in the Elizabethan audiences would recognise and appreciate
Shakespeare's use of the language and themes of sonnets in the play.
For example, they would recognise that Rosaline is the beautiful but
unavailable woman of so many sonnets. She is the 'lady' who makes
Laura like 'a kitchen wench'. Even the final six lines of the play would
be heard as echoing the final stanza and couplet of a sonnet:

> A glooming peace this morning with it brings,
> The sun for sorrow will not show his head.
> Go hence to have more talk of these sad things;
> Some shall be pardoned, and some punishèd:
> For never was a story of more woe
> Than this of Juliet and her Romeo.   *(Act 5 Scene 3, lines 305–10)*

Tragedy

Romeo and Juliet can also be understood in the context of the
Elizabethan appetite for revenge tragedy. Audiences flocked to such
plays; it was a highly popular genre. Shakespeare had already written
one bloodsoaked revenge tragedy in the early 1590s: *Titus Andronicus*.

The public demand that existed for such plays provides a general reason why Shakespeare wrote *Romeo and Juliet*: it had great box-office appeal. The audience recognised Romeo the lover transformed into a revenger by the death of Mercutio. His vengeance, killing Tybalt, accelerates the tragic action of the play.

But with the creation of *Romeo and Juliet*, Shakespeare began to change the nature of tragedy itself, expanding it beyond classical conceptions of tragedy and the blood-boltered melodramas of the early 1590s. Earlier tragedies had nearly always dealt with the downfall of great men: kings or powerful nobles (Titus Andronicus is a famous general of Rome). Such traditional tragedies portrayed the destruction of the mighty, and the consequences for the state of their death. But Romeo and Juliet are quite different. They are young and innocent. They possess no power, and are unable to influence matters of state. Theirs is a domestic tragedy, and it takes place in a play that mixes comedy into the tragic pattern.

Shakespeare may have been redefining the genre of tragedy with *Romeo and Juliet*, but he ensured that conventionally expected tragic elements were present in the play. Although the central characters are unlike the powerful high-status characters of traditional tragedy, their story does show fortune's turning wheel as they decline from happiness through suffering to death. Like any classical tragedy, theirs is a story of waste, of irretrievable and poignant loss. Although critics are divided on what causes their deaths (Is it a character flaw, or the cruel working of fate and mischance, or some social cause like the feud or patriarchy?), the young lovers' story is undoubtedly tragic in the sense of young lives destroyed by powers outside their control.

Romeo and Juliet can also be considered in the context of Shakespeare's writing career. He seems to have been particularly fascinated by the theme of a father's opposition to his daughter's desire to marry. He had first explored that theme in an early play, *The Two Gentlemen of Verona*. But Shakespeare was a restless experimenter, and he moved on to extend his dramatic examination of the same theme of father–daughter conflict in two very different plays, *A Midsummer Night's Dream* and *Romeo and Juliet* (no one knows if he wrote *Dream* before or after *Romeo and Juliet*).

There is a further thematic similarity between the two plays. *A Midsummer Night's Dream* contains the Mechanicals' production of the story of Pyramus and Thisbe. That story has a remarkable resemblance to that of *Romeo and Juliet*. In both, lovers from feuding families kill themselves, neither wishing to live without the other. Mistakes play a key part in their deaths. But in *Dream*, the Mechanicals' performance of the lovers' death scene is a parody, intended to make the audience laugh. In *Romeo and Juliet*, such laughter would be out of place. Within a very short time, in the mid 1590s, Shakespeare created two dramatic versions of young lovers threatened by parental rage. One emerged as comedy, the other as tragedy. *A Midsummer Night's Dream* ends happily in marriage; *Romeo and Juliet* ends unhappily in death.

What was Shakespeare's England like?

Shakespeare's audiences, watching performances of *Romeo and Juliet*, would recognise certain aspects of their own world. Many of those recognitions were of minor, taken-for-granted features of Elizabethan life. The rowdy servants who open the play, foul-mouthed and looking for a fight, were a common sight on London's streets. Capulet's masked dance resembles festivities in affluent Elizabethan households. Lady Capulet's elaborate comparison of Paris to a book (Act 1 Scene 3, lines 82–93) was a familiar reminder of the clasps and bindings of contemporary expensive volumes. In Act 5 Scene 1, Romeo's description of the Apothecary's shop would recall similar shops which the playgoers saw daily as they walked around the city.

Other reflections of English society in the 1590s abound. The intense male friendships evident in the play were customary among Elizabethan men. Listening to Mercutio's mocking of fashionable Italian sword-fencing styles ('passado', 'punto reverso'), the audience would be reminded of the popular fencing schools which flourished in London, teaching those very techniques. The Nurse's talk of how her bones ache, and Mercutio's mention of blistered lips in his Queen Mab speech, could be recognised as symptoms of the sexually-transmitted diseases that affected many Elizabethans. Some critics have even claimed that Prince Escales would remind Shakespeare's audiences of Queen Elizabeth, arguing that both rulers' apparent firmness concealed an underlying tendency to procrastinate and avoid conflict with powerful factions.

Beyond such topical reminders of everyday life there are deeper ways in which *Romeo and Juliet* reveals what Elizabethan England was like. What follows identifies important social and cultural contexts that influenced the creation of *Romeo and Juliet*: concerns about feuding and violence, the Elizabethan household and patriarchal authority, children and sexual maturity, the plague, religion, contempt for foreigners, and attitudes to death.

Feuding and violence

The feuding of the Montagues and Capulets reflects a well-known aspect of Elizabethan England: violence was commonplace. Duelling was a familiar practice; even the playwrights Jonson and Marlowe were each involved in duels. But duels were usually very personal affairs. More far-reaching in their consequences were feuds between factions of the aristocracy. The Elizabethan upper class was notorious for its quarrels and vendettas because as upper-class families struggled to gain more wealth, power and prestige, they offended other families. The result was a smouldering animosity of household against household.

It needed only the tiny sparks of trivial incidents to ignite the enmity into violence, which sometimes resulted in deaths. Throughout Elizabeth's reign there were numerous vicious clashes. On some occasions there were pitched battles in the streets between servants or supporters of rival factions. Proclamations against public brawling showed that the authorities were alarmed by the intensity and frequency of such disputes. Prince Escales' angry rebuke to the feuding families in the play's first scene ('Rebellious subjects, enemies to peace') would sound familiar to the ears of Shakespeare's audience. The historian Robert Lacey, in his book *Robert, Earl of Essex*, comments:

> In such an age of naked brutality and casual bloodshed it was no coincidence that Shakespeare's plays should centre on personally inflicted acts of justice and revenge: the feud between the Montagues and Capulets came from life in London of the 1590s where 'cutters' and 'hacksters' could make a good living selling their villainous services.

The Elizabethan household and patriarchal authority

The play provides lively portrayals of private life in a wealthy upper-middle-class family. As noted on page 59, *Romeo and Juliet* is a domestic tragedy. Its characters are not the powerful kings or warriors of traditional tragedy, but the leading citizens of an Italian city, rich but not aristocratic. The domestic setting reveals significant aspects of affluent households in early modern England.

In Act 1 Scene 5, servants bustle about in preparation for the dancing that follows a meal. They scrape wooden dishes on which the food was served ('trenchers'), rearrange the furniture, make sure they save some of the guests' food for themselves, and arrange for their own entertainment later that night ('let the porter let in Susan Grindstone and Nell'). Like an Elizabethan host, Capulet gives the servants orders to provide more light, shift the tables and damp down the fire because the room has become too hot.

In Act 4, as Capulet prepares for Juliet's wedding breakfast, the talk is of baked meats, spices, dates and quinces. The servants bring in logs and baskets, and metal spits on which to roast the meat. The atmosphere is very like that of the activity of an affluent Elizabethan family as it excitedly prepares for a marriage, with the head of the family showing clearly that he is in charge:

> Make haste, make haste. Sirrah, fetch drier logs.
> . . .
> Nurse! Wife! What ho! What, Nurse, I say!
> Go waken Juliet, go and trim her up,
> I'll go and chat with Paris. Hie, make haste
>
> *(Act 4 Scene 4, lines 16–26)*

Here, Capulet appears an affable if fussy head of the household, but his earlier treatment of Juliet reveals a far less benign aspect of Veronese – and Elizabethan – society. In Shakespeare's time, husbands and fathers strictly controlled the lives of wives and daughters. *Romeo and Juliet* reflects the subordinate position of women in Elizabethan England. Women had limited personal autonomy; their status and roles were subject to the tyranny of patriarchy (rule by men). Their rights were restricted, legally, socially and economically.

You can find a more extended discussion of the consequences of such gender discrimination on pages 93–7 under feminist criticism. Here it needs to be said that Elizabethans widely accepted that the husband and father should rule the family, just as a monarch reigned over the state, and God held dominion over all.

Religion was a powerful instrument to enforce the belief of male superiority. The Elizabethan *Homily of the State of Matrimony* was frequently read aloud in church. It ordered wives to obey their husbands, and instructed husbands that 'the woman is a frail vessel and thou art therefore made the ruler and head over her'. That domination extended even more powerfully over female children, particularly with regard to marriage. Daughters were regarded as possessions, to be traded as the father saw fit in a marriage settlement which would benefit his family. Capulet puts this patriarchal assumption in its starkest form as he declares his rights over his daughter:

> And you be mine, I'll give you to my friend
>
> *(Act 3 Scene 5, line 191)*

The line is also revealing about the position of children in Elizabethan society. Sons and daughters were expected to be obedient to their parents' will, particularly their father's. But it would be wrong to assume that fathers had absolute power and invariably acted as tyrants. There is much evidence that in practice children had a say over who they married, and that good relationships existed in many families. Few fathers imposed their will rigidly. Capulet acknowledges this early in the play when he urges Paris to woo Juliet, but seems to suggest that her consent to the proposal is vital. He implies that his daughter has some choice in her marriage partner:

> My will to her consent is but a part;
> And she agreed, within her scope of choice
> Lies my consent and fair according voice.
>
> *(Act 1 Scene 2, lines 17–19)*

Nonetheless, during the 1590s the questions of a daughter's right to choose her own husband and her duty to obey her father were much discussed topics. The interest that Shakespeare's contemporaries had in such matters is evident in his plays. He explored the issues, so evident in Juliet's dilemma, throughout his entire playwriting career. As noted on page 59, in *A Midsummer Night's Dream* another daughter, Hermia, is threatened by her father, who calls for her death if she will not marry the man of his choice. Other variations on the theme of fathers seeking to control their daughters' lives are found in

The Two Gentlemen of Verona, *The Merchant of Venice*, *Much Ado About Nothing*, *As You Like It*, *The Merry Wives of Windsor*, *Hamlet*, *Othello*, *King Lear*, *Cymbeline*, *The Winter's Tale* and *The Tempest*. All reflect the interest in Shakespeare's time in the extent of patriarchal power: how far children should obey their fathers. That such obedience was customarily expected and received is shown in the comment of the historian Lawrence Stone. He argues that an Elizabethan audience saw the tragedy of Romeo and Juliet

> not so much in their ill-starred romance as in the way they
> brought destruction upon themselves by violating the norms of
> the society in which they lived

Those norms applied to every aspect of behaviour. Just as the man was at the head of the family, so the family was at the centre of social life. Conduct was governed by a web of complex and demanding expectations and conventions. Romeo and Juliet transgress one such social rule by marrying secretly. In Elizabethan England, every well-off family would have a forthcoming marriage very formally announced in church. The process of 'calling the banns' meant that the intended marriage was declared publicly on three successive Sundays. The wedding itself would be one of great celebration, with religious and social ceremonies that involved both families and their friends. By having the lovers flout social convention by marrying so hastily and clandestinely, Shakespeare creates audience expectation that calamity will surely follow.

Children and sexual maturity

The play also reveals aspects of Elizabethan practices and attitudes to children and childrearing. The Nurse's tale of putting wormwood on her nipple to wean Juliet reflects contemporary breastfeeding practices. Many wealthy households employed 'wet nurses', women paid to breastfeed the babies of the mistress of the house. Such women, often of low status, remained in the house and developed close bonds with the growing child. That relationship is portrayed in the Nurse's evident affection for Juliet.

Much more significant for Shakespeare's contemporaries was the question of Juliet's age. She would seem very young to an Elizabethan audience, certainly far too young to marry. In the 1590s, men and women usually married in their mid to late twenties. To marry younger than 20 was uncommon, whatever the social status of the partners. Even among the poor, some degree of economic security was expected, at least for the male. So in making Juliet only 13, Shakespeare was raising questions of social propriety. It was not considered decent to marry so young. Even today, a 13-year-old marrying makes front page news and, as shown on page 99, in the eighteenth century David Garrick's version of the play (which held the stage for 100 years) made Juliet 18 in order to avoid criticism of her character.

The question of appropriate social conduct for a young girl has been relevant throughout every age. The Elizabethans would not only be disquieted by Juliet's marriage, they would be especially shocked by her behaviour. It was quite beyond the bounds of accepted conduct for a 13-year-old to kiss on first meeting, to express impatience to lose her virginity, and to look forward to sexual pleasure. The fact that Juliet was played by a young male actor might well have heightened the impact on Elizabethan audiences.

Juliet would be familiar to Shakespeare's contemporaries as a young girl in a prosperous family like so many in their own society. She is kept under close control, and has to ask permission to go out, even to go to church for confession. In such ways, Juliet conforms to expected rules for conduct. But for one so young to express sexual desire so openly, to disobey and deceive her parents so wilfully, demonstrated behaviour of which Elizabethans strongly disapproved. Contemporary ideas of femininity and youth valued submissiveness and modesty. By making Juliet only 13, Shakespeare increased the dramatic impact of his story and raised issues of immediate relevance to his audience.

The plague

Mercutio's dying curse, 'A plague a'both your houses!', held additional meaning for the play's original audiences. So too did Friar John's tale in Act 5 Scene 2 of the 'infectious pestilence' which prevented him from delivering the letter that might have saved the lives of Romeo and Juliet. In 1593–4, only a year or so before the first performance of the play, a severe outbreak of plague had closed all the theatres in London. For all Londoners, the plague was a constant threat. Almost every member of the audience watching the play would have been affected in some way by the plague. They would know some friend, neighbour or family member who had fallen victim to the epidemics which occurred all too frequently in England, disrupting normal life. For Elizabethans, the plague gave a curious and unnatural relevance to the tragedy: it was yet another cause of children dying before their parents, just as in the play Montague and Capulet outlive Romeo and Juliet.

Religion

The religious beliefs of Elizabethan England pervade the play. Its language abounds in 'religious' words: 'heaven', 'heretics', 'mass', 'angel', 'God' are just a few of many such terms. Romeo and Juliet's first conversation is an extended conceit (image) that compares Juliet to a shrine or saint. Its vocabulary draws extensively upon Christianity: 'profane', 'sin', 'devotion', 'prayer', etc. Elizabethans would be completely familiar with the notion of pilgrims making long journeys to the shrines of the Holy Land in order to demonstrate their faith. They would know that pilgrims brought back palm leaves as proof of their visits, and so were known as 'palmers':

ROMEO   If I profane with my unworthiest hand
          This holy shrine, the gentle sin is this,
          My lips, two blushing pilgrims, ready stand
          To smooth that rough touch with a tender kiss.
JULIET   Good pilgrim, you do wrong your hand too much,
          Which mannerly devotion shows in this,
          For saints have hands that pilgrims' hands do touch,
          And palm to palm is holy palmers' kiss.
ROMEO   Have not saints lips, and holy palmers too?
JULIET   Ay, pilgrim, lips that they must use in prayer.
ROMEO   O then, dear saint, let lips do what hands do:
          They pray, grant thou, lest faith turn to despair.
JULIET   Saints do not move, though grant for prayers' sake.
ROMEO   Then move not while my prayer's effect I take.
          Thus from my lips, by thine, my sin is purged.
                    [Kissing her.]
JULIET   Then have my lips the sin that they have took.
ROMEO   Sin from my lips? O trespass sweetly urged!
          Give me my sin again.
                    [Kissing her again.]   (Act 1 Scene 5, lines 92–109)

Many members of a modern audience are not aware of all the religious connotations of the dialogue, but to Elizabethans such associations were everyday knowledge. Early modern England was a profoundly religious country. Religion utterly dominated most people's lives in ways which it can be difficult to identify with today. Virtually everybody in England cared passionately about religion. It was ever present, a source of both comfort and anxiety.

Because religion pervaded almost every aspect of Elizabethan life, it is not surprising that *Romeo and Juliet* bears evidence of its influence. The English language was itself permeated with the language of religion. But Shakespeare added extra religious resonance by setting the tragedy in Catholic Italy, a society that was regarded with extreme suspicion by the Protestants who probably made up the majority of Elizabethan theatre audiences. Since Henry VIII's break with Rome in the 1530s, with the exception of the six-year reign of Queen Mary, England had been a Protestant country. Two major aspects of *Romeo and Juliet* would feed Protestant prejudices about foreign Catholics: the Franciscan priest, Friar Lawrence, and the lovers' suicide.

For Shakespeare's contemporaries, the very fact that he is a friar made Lawrence someone not to be trusted. In English folk tales, friars had long been characterised as figures of fun, full of human weaknesses. They were held up to ridicule for their deceit, hypocrisy and depravity. Friars were portrayed as secretly lustful, and addicted to all kinds of sly plots and stratagems. In this sense, Elizabethans were predisposed to seeing Friar Lawrence as the meddlesome friar of tradition.

However, Protestantism, with its antagonism to all things Catholic, intensified that attitude, giving it sinister undertones. Many Elizabethans saw in Friar Lawrence their stereotype of the scheming Italian priest. Their jaundiced preconception would be confirmed by his actions, most obviously the way he readily breaks church law in secretly conducting the marriage of a 13-year-old girl, and then deceives her parents with a dangerous plan of his own devising.

Few interpretations today regard Shakespeare's Friar as like that simple stereotype. He is seen as a complex character, who in some modern productions assumes great significance. It should also be remarked that some productions fruitfully exploit the play's religious aspects to create atmosphere and to provide characters with a 'past' that adds to their complexity. For example, Baz Luhrmann's film vividly incorporates Catholic symbolism. Images of the Madonna abound, Juliet's room is filled with religious icons, and in the closing scene she lies in a vast cathedral, brilliantly lit by the thousands of candles that surround her.

Elizabethans would also see significance in the lovers' suicide. All of Shakespeare's contemporaries worried about the state of their souls, about sin, and about what would happen after death. The question of salvation obsessed them: would they go to heaven or hell? Many would be shocked by the suicide of the lovers. Suicide was condemned by the church as against God's will, and suicides were believed to go straight to hell. It is possible that for Protestants the shock at the lovers' suicide would be lessened by the setting: Catholic Italy. They believed, as the following section shows, that in Italy all kinds of 'unnatural' things went on.

Contempt for foreigners

Shakespeare lived at a time when England was rapidly becoming more wealthy as it expanded its possessions abroad. With that expansion, often through conquest, came a growing sense of national identity. But as they felt more secure in themselves as a nation, the English developed unflattering or contemptuous views of foreigners. Italy and Italians suffered particularly from this Elizabethan stereotyping. The popular attitude of the time to Italy was often that of scorn and ridicule. It was a place where all kinds of 'unnatural' things were perpetrated: murder, lust and vice of all kinds. In reality, 'unnatural' meant things that were thought to be 'unEnglish'.

Italy was seen as a corrupt country, where treachery and perversion flourished. Italians were regarded by many English men and women as deceitful, unreliable and vengeful, always working out treacherous plots and intrigues. Some of the roots of that suspicion lay in religion, particularly the anti-Catholicism fostered by King Henry VIII's break with Rome. But it was fuelled by all kinds of contemporary propaganda. Here, for example, is Thomas Nashe, writing in the 1590s:

> O Italy, the Academy of manslaughter, the sporting place of murder, the Apothecary shop of poison for all nations: how many kinds of weapons hast thou invented for malice?

Nashe's condemnation echoes that of Roger Ascham, who had been tutor to Princess Elizabeth before she became Queen. In *The Schoolmaster* (1570) he wrote of Italy:

> sin by lust and vanity, hath and doth breed up everywhere common contempt of God's word, private contention in many families, open factions in every city.

Ascham's comment on 'factions' refers to the frequent blood feuds for which Italy was notorious. Frederick R Bryson in *The Sixteenth-Century Duel* gives an account of one such Italian feud:

> In 1567 a private battle was fought at Sassoferrato. The origin of the dissension was the loan of a small sum by Jofo Baroni to a son of Meo Jani. From an ensuing dispute there arose between the families Jani and Calderani a feud which in the course of time led to the death of fourteen men and two young women; the latter were both killed in a duel for which they had each challenged each other.

Knowledge of such feuds (albeit in garbled form) and the prejudices exhibited by Nashe and Ascham were the kinds of popular belief that help explain Elizabethan and Jacobean enthusiasm for dramatic portrayals of corrupt Italians. Jacobean tragedies such as John Webster's *The White Devil* and *The Duchess of Malfi* are extreme examples of the genre that so appealed to English prejudices. *Romeo and Juliet* is not usually thought of together with such biased depictions. But the play's recurring violence, the emotional ferocity of some of its characters, a shockingly under-age heroine, together with a scheming friar are among its features which appealed to Elizabethan preconceptions of Italy as a place of extreme passions and sexual licence.

Death

Romeo and Juliet, a play centrally concerned with love, seems equally preoccupied with death. At several points, Juliet is imagined as Death's bride (see examples on page 77), and just before she drinks the potion she fantasises about lying in the Capulet tomb surrounded by the rotting corpses of her ancestors.

Such apparently morbid fixations did not seem bizarre or ghoulish to Shakespeare's contemporaries. They regarded death and decay in ways that western society today finds unfamiliar, and often abhorrent. Elizabethans looked human mortality squarely in the face. Disease and death were ever-present for most families. The average life expectancy was little more than 30 years, there was a high infant death rate and, as noted above, the plague was a regular visitor to city and country alike.

With death such a familiar experience, it found all kinds of everyday expression. Bones and skulls frequently figured in paintings and woodcuts. Tomb sculptures often portrayed the physical signs of human decay, sometimes presenting two versions of the dead person: one richly clothed as in life, the other a mere skeleton. People kept, or gave each other, *memento mori*: reminders of mortality, like small carved death's heads. Most English churchyards contained a charnel-house. It was a building where bones and skulls were stacked after they were dug up when fresh graves were being prepared for new burials. Juliet's description of what she would rather do than marry Paris was instantly understandable by Shakespeare's audiences:

> Or hide me nightly in a charnel-house,
> O'ercovered quite with dead men's rattling bones,
> With reeky shanks and yellow chapless skulls;
> Or bid me go into a new-made grave,
> And hide me with a dead man in his shroud

(Act 4 Scene 1, lines 81–5)

Rituals associated with death were highly important to the Elizabethans. The mourning around the 'dead' Juliet (Act 4 Scene 5, lines 14–64) often sounds excessive to modern ears, and is claimed by some critics to reveal only false emotion (see page 40). But these ritualised expressions of grief probably did not sound strange or insincere to Shakespeare's contemporaries. Similarly, they would recognise familiar funeral practices in the promise of Capulet and Montague to set up golden statues to their children. It was customary for wealthy families to erect elaborate monuments to the dead. Many such memorials can still be seen in English churches.

Shakespeare's own life

This section began with the film *Shakespeare in Love*, which is a delightful fantasy, giving the impression that the inspiration for *Romeo and Juliet* was Shakespeare's own personal experience of falling in love. Today, critics and examiners give little or no credit to approaches which interpret *Romeo and Juliet* in the context of Shakespeare's emotional life, because nothing is really known of his intimate thoughts, feelings or activities. Nonetheless some critics have made such a claim. For example, E K Chambers wrote in 1904 that the play

> reflects something of that disturbance in Shakespeare's own
> emotional life, of which the more direct record is in the
> Sonnets . . . As he sees love, in the distorted glass of his own
> unlucky experience, it is of the essence that it should issue
> tragically.

Such a claim is simply not provable (or disprovable!). Today the focus of critical attention is on the social and cultural contexts discussed in this chapter. An important critical question concerns Shakespeare's attitude to such contexts: what was his personal view of the practices, conventions and values of the time? For example, is his portrayal of patriarchy ironic and subversive, or is the play an endorsement of male power? Again, the truth of the matter is that no one really knows, but as shown throughout this Guide, and particularly in the section on Critical approaches, it is possible to construct persuasive arguments to support almost any interpretation of how the play challenges or supports aspects of Elizabethan England.

Recently, one aspect has gained academic respectability: the notion that Shakespeare was a secret Catholic, and that there is evidence of his Catholicism in the plays. Throughout Shakespeare's life, England was a Protestant country, and many English people faced persecution and death for remaining faithful to Catholicism ('the old religion'). The argument goes that Shakespeare had to be extremely cautious not to be discovered, but he showed his adherence to Catholicism in the plays. There is not space here to set out the carefully argued case that some modern scholars use to support this theory, but you can find a good account in E A G Honigmann's, *Shakespeare: the 'Lost Years'* (1985).

Expressions from *Romeo and Juliet* have become universally known. They are used in all kinds of discourse: 'O Romeo, Romeo, wherefore art thou Romeo?', 'What's in a name?', 'star-crossed lovers', 'on a wild goose chase', 'A plague on both your houses', 'A rose by any other word would smell as sweet', and many others.

But the language of the play is much more than a treasure-house of quotations. It contains a dazzling variety of language registers. Its stylistic diversity can be seen by simply listing a few of its types: lyrical poetry, witty and sophisticated wordplay in both prose and verse (see page oo), highly patterned rhyme and rhythm, colloquial language, literary and classical references, violent exclamations, artificial conceits and sincere expressions of love, sonnets, hyperbole and impassioned rhetoric. The language of tender love is counterpoised by bawdy: the recurring sexual innuendo which constantly subverts the ideal of romantic love.

Ben Jonson famously remarked that Shakespeare 'wanted art' (lacked technical skill). But his comment is mistaken, as is the popular image of Shakespeare as a 'natural' writer, utterly spontaneous, inspired only by his imagination. Shakespeare possessed a profound knowledge of the language techniques of his own and previous times. Behind the apparently effortless flow of language lies a deeply practised skill. The play is not only about love, it also shows Shakespeare's love of language. What follows are some of the language techniques he uses in *Romeo and Juliet* to intensify dramatic effect, create mood and character, and so produce memorable theatre. As you read them, always keep in mind that Shakespeare wrote for the stage, and that actors will therefore employ a wide variety of both verbal and non-verbal methods to exploit the dramatic possibilities of the language. They will use the full range of their voices and accompany the words with appropriate expressions, gestures and actions.

Antithesis

Antithesis is the opposition of words or phrases against each other, as in 'Here's much to do with hate, but more with love' (Act 1 Scene 1, line 166), 'More light and light, more dark and dark our woes!' (Act 3 Scene 5, line 36). This setting of word against word ('hate' versus 'love', 'light' versus 'dark') is one of Shakespeare's favourite language devices. He uses it extensively in all his plays. Why? Because antithesis powerfully expresses conflict through its use of opposites, and conflict is the essence of all drama.

In *Romeo and Juliet*, conflict occurs in many forms: Montague versus Capulet, youth versus age, life versus death, the bridal bed versus the grave, appearance versus reality and, as above, love versus hate and light versus dark. Antithesis intensifies that sense of conflict, and embodies its different forms. For example, Friar Lawrence's first speech contains at least 15 antitheses in 30 lines as he gathers plants and ponders on the potential for good and evil in every living thing. He begins with two antitheses in his first line, 'The grey-eyed morn smiles on the frowning night', and by using many other powerful oppositions ('baleful weeds' against 'precious-juiced flowers', 'tomb' against 'womb', 'virtue' against 'vice', and so on), he works up to his conclusion:

> Two such opposèd kings encamp them still
> In man as well as herbs, grace and rude will
>
> *(Act 2 Scene 3, lines 27–8)*

In another speech full of sharply contrasting antitheses, Capulet grieves for Juliet. He contrasts the happy preparations for the intended wedding with the mourning rites that now must mark her death:

> All things that we ordainèd festival,
> Turn from their office to black funeral:
> Our instruments to melancholy bells,
> Our wedding cheer to a sad burial feast;
> Our solemn hymns to sullen dirges change;
> Our bridal flowers serve for a buried corse;
> And all things change them to the contrary.
>
> *(Act 4 Scene 5, lines 84–90)*

A special kind of antithesis that Shakespeare uses in the play is oxymoron. Here, two incongruous or contradictory words are placed next to each other to make a striking expression, as in 'cold fire' or 'bright smoke'. At the end of the 'balcony' scene, Juliet uses a memorable oxymoron to describe her feelings: 'Parting is such sweet sorrow'. Oxymoron comes from two Greek words: *oxys* ('sharp'), and *moros* ('dull'). Oxymorons bring out even more sharply the sense of oppositions in the play. Romeo, on his first appearance, seeing the signs of the brawl, speaks a dozen oxymorons as he reflects on love and hate:

> Why then, O brawling love, O loving hate,
> O any thing of nothing first create!
> O heavy lightness, serious vanity,
> Misshapen chaos of well-seeming forms,
> Feather of lead, bright smoke, cold fire, sick health,
> Still-waking sleep, that is not what it is!

> *(Act 1 Scene 1, lines 167–72)*

Imagery

Romeo and Juliet abounds in imagery: vivid words and phrases that help create the atmosphere of the play as they conjure up emotionally-charged pictures in the imagination. For example, the Prologue describes the lovers as 'star-crossed' and their love as 'death-marked'. As both a poet and a playwright, Shakespeare seems to have thought in images, and the whole play richly demonstrates his unflagging and varied use of verbal illustration.

Early critics such as Doctor Johnson and John Dryden were critical of Shakespeare's fondness for imagery. They felt that many images obscured meaning and detracted attention from the subjects they represented. But over the past two hundred years, critics, poets and audiences have increasingly valued Shakespeare's imagery (sometimes called 'figures' or 'figurative language'). They recognise how he uses it to give pleasure as it stirs the audience's imagination, deepens the dramatic impact of particular moments or moods, provides insight into character, and intensifies meaning and emotional force. Images carry powerful significance far deeper than their surface meanings.

A striking example of Shakespeare's use of imagery is at the moment when Juliet learns that Romeo, her husband, has killed Tybalt, her cousin. She struggles to express her contradictory feelings for Romeo: how could such a beloved, beautiful person commit so vile a deed; how could such beautiful reality cover such malicious reality? Her mind is entirely on Romeo and, experiencing violently opposing emotions, she describes him in what Russ McDonald calls 'a blizzard of images'. Her long list of antitheses and oxymorons reveals Shakespeare's infinitely fertile imagination at work to provide Juliet with more than a dozen images to express her conflicting perceptions of Romeo:

> O serpent heart, hid with a flow'ring face!
> Did ever dragon keep so fair a cave?
> Beautiful tyrant, fiend angelical!
> Dove-feathered raven, wolvish-ravening lamb!
> Despisèd substance of divinest show!
> Just opposite to what thou justly seem'st,
> A damnèd saint, an honourable villain!
> O nature, what hadst thou to do in hell
> When thou didst bower the spirit of a fiend
> In mortal paradise of such sweet flesh?
> Was ever book containing such vile matter
> So fairly bound? O that deceit should dwell
> In such a gorgeous palace!   *(Act 3 Scene 2, lines 73–85)*

Juliet's cascading images (serpent, flower, dragon, cave, fiend, etc.) are typical of the profusion of such word pictures throughout the play. Caroline Spurgeon, the critic who pioneered the study of Shakespeare's imagery (see pages 86–7), counted over 200 images in *Romeo and Juliet*. She noted that a number of images recurred ('iterative imagery'), helping to create a sense of the themes of the play. One such image cluster is that of light and dark, which includes the following examples used by the lovers about each other:

> O she doth teach the torches to burn bright!
> It seems she hangs upon the cheek of night
> As a rich jewel in an Ethiop's ear   *(Act 1 Scene 5, lines 43–5)*

> The brightness of her cheek would shame those stars,
> As daylight doth a lamp   *(Act 2 Scene 2, lines 19–20)*

> Take him and cut him out in little stars,
> And he will make the face of heaven so fine
> That all the world will be in love with night,
> And pay no worship to the garish sun.
>
> *(Act 3 Scene 2, lines 22–5)*

> For here lies Juliet, and her beauty makes
> This vault a feasting presence full of light.
>
> *(Act 5 Scene 3, lines 85–6)*

Some of the play's images appear to be highly embroidered and extravagant comparisons. Such images are often referred to as 'conceits', a term which has come to imply a negative evaluation. George Bernard Shaw, for example, spoke of the 'silly lyrical conceits which were the foible of the Elizabethans'. One conceit frequently singled out for criticism is Lady Capulet's advice to Juliet to marry Paris, comparing him to a book which Juliet should read:

> Read o'er the volume of young Paris' face,
> And find delight writ there with beauty's pen
>
> *(Act 1 Scene 3, lines 82–4)*

Her conceit is spun out, sonnet-like, over 14 lines. It is often judged as showy and ornamental, and so portraying insincerity rather than genuine emotions. Sometimes it is regarded as Shakespeare self-indulgently showing off his language skills to convey the impression of Lady Capulet 'selling' Paris to her daughter. Such judgements are open to argument, but what is not disputed is that Shakespeare's imagery uses metaphor, simile or personification. All are comparisons which in effect substitute one thing (the image) for another (the thing described).

- A *simile* compares one thing to another, using 'like' or 'as'; for example, 'shrieks like mandrakes' torn out of the earth', and 'My bounty is as boundless as the sea, / My love as deep'.
- A *metaphor* is also a comparison, suggesting that two dissimilar things are actually the same. When Romeo says 'O speak again, bright angel' he implies that Juliet is an angel, some glorious thing to be praised. To put it another way, a metaphor borrows one word

or phrase to express another, for example when Benvolio uses 'piercing steel' to mean Tybalt's sword.

- *Personification* turns all kinds of things into persons, giving them human feelings or attributes. Capulet uses personification when he describes the coming of spring as 'When well-apparelled April on the heel / Of limping winter treads' (Act 1 Scene 2, lines 27–8). Probably the most powerful personification in the play is the image of Death as Juliet's husband, which recurs in different forms:

> And death, not Romeo, take my maidenhead!
>
> *(Act 3 Scene 2, line 137)*

> I would the fool were married to her grave.
>
> *(Act 3 Scene 5, line 140)*

> Death is my son-in-law, Death is my heir,
> My daughter he hath wedded.   *(Act 4 Scene 5, lines 38–9)*

> Shall I believe
> That unsubstantial Death is amorous,
> And that the lean abhorrèd monster keeps
> Thee here in dark to be his paramour?
>
> *(Act 5 Scene 3, lines 102–5)*

Repetition

Repetitions run through the play, contributing to its emotional climate and dramatic impact. Apart from familiar grammatical words ('the', 'and', etc.) the two lexical words most frequently repeated are 'love' (used over 130 times) and 'death' (around 70 times). Their repetition is a clear indication of two of the play's major themes or concerns.

In the same way, the recurrence throughout the play of words to do with time creates the sense of that theme or leitmotif: 'day', 'night', 'years', 'hours', 'minutes', 'today', 'tomorrow', etc. The words intensify the impression of the gathering pace of the drama, suggesting the rush of events that overwhelm the lovers. Shakespeare packs Act 3 Scene 4 with such 'time' words, to convey the pressure building up on Juliet at that particular point in the play (see page 32).

Shakespeare's skill in using repetition to heighten theatrical effect and deepen emotional and imaginative significance is most evident in particular speeches. Repeated words, phrases, rhythms and sounds add intensity to the moment or episode. For example, as Juliet eagerly awaits Romeo and speaks her *epithalamium*, or wedding song, the urgent repetitions of 'night' and 'come' express her passionate longing for Romeo:

> Come, Night, come, Romeo, come, thou day in night,
> For thou wilt lie upon the wings of night,
> Whiter than new snow upon a raven's back.
> Come, gentle Night, come, loving, black-browed Night
>
> *(Act 3 Scene 2, lines 17–20)*

Juliet's lines also reveal the Elizabethans' delight in assonance, the repetition of vowel sounds. Poets and playwrights of the time took particular pleasure in playing with such sounds, often in ways that sound artificial today. A striking example is Juliet's repetition of the 'I', 'ay' and 'eye' sound when she mistakes the Nurse's grief as implying that Romeo is dead:

> Say thou but 'ay',
> And that bare vowel 'I' shall poison more
> Than the death-darting eye of cockatrice.
> I am not I, if there be such an 'ay',
> Or those eyes shut, that makes thee answer 'ay'.
>
> *(Act 3 Scene 2, lines 45–9)*

In Act 4 Scene 5, lines 34–64, a similar wealth of repetitions of words and sounds is evident in the mourning of the Capulets, the Nurse and Paris over the 'dead' Juliet ('O day, O day, O day, O hateful day!'). As mentioned earlier, the lamentations are also often regarded as contrived and false by modern standards. For that reason they are often heavily cut in production (as are Juliet's words above). But around the time that Shakespeare wrote the play, this highly patterned formal language was considered appropriate to such scenes.

Sometimes phrases are repeated to give emphasis to argument, as in Friar Lawrence's threefold repetition of 'there art thou happy' as he rebukes Romeo and reminds him of his good fortune (Act 3 Scene 3, lines 135–40). On other occasions the form of a speech is repeated, as for example when Juliet responds to her mother's alarming news of imminent marriage to Paris. The parallel form of Juliet's reply has several dramatic functions. It increases the tightening tension of the plot, reveals Juliet's determined resolution, and can, if Juliet chooses, evoke audience laughter:

LADY CAPULET   The County Paris, at Saint Peter's Church,
        Shall happily make thee there a joyful bride.
JULIET   Now by Saint Peter's Church and Peter too,
        He shall not make me there a joyful bride.

                            (Act 3 Scene 5, lines 114–17)

Repetition also occurs in rhyme, which is used to achieve different effects. For example, all of Act 2 Scene 3 is in rhyming couplets, perhaps to highlight the moralistic tone of Friar Lawrence's reflections on nature and, in his conversation with Romeo, to contrast with the free-flowing lyricism of the blank verse (unrhymed) of the 'balcony' scene which has just preceded this scene. Elsewhere, a rhyming couplet is sometimes used to give a distinctive ending to an episode or scene, or to the play itself:

    For never was a story of more woe
    Than this of Juliet and her Romeo.

                            (Act 5 Scene 3, lines 309–10)

Lists

One of Shakespeare's favourite language methods is to accumulate words or phrases rather like a list. He had learned the technique as a schoolboy in Stratford-upon-Avon, and his skill in knowing how to use lists dramatically is evident in the many examples in *Romeo and Juliet*. He intensifies and varies description, atmosphere and argument as he 'piles up' item on item, incident on incident. Sometimes the list comprises only single words, as in Capulet's mourning for Juliet ('Despised, distressed, hated, martyred, killed!'), or in his exasperation when she defies him:

    God's bread, it makes me mad! Day, night, work, play,
    Alone, in company, still my care hath been
    To have her matched   *(Act 3 Scene 5, lines 176–8)*

Other lists build up a detailed description, as in Mercutio's freewheeling portrayal of Queen Mab and her effects on sleepers (Act 1 Scene 4, lines 54–95). Similar descriptive lists include Romeo's depiction of the Apothecary and his shop (Act 5 Scene 1, lines 37–48), and the many images in his characterisation of love:

> Love is a smoke made with the fume of sighs,
> Being purged, a fire sparkling in lovers' eyes,
> Being vexed, a sea nourished with loving tears.
> What is it else? a madness most discreet,
> A choking gall, and a preserving sweet.
>
> *(Act 1 Scene 1, lines 181–5)*

Other notable examples include the list of persons invited to the Capulets' party, which ends with the intriguing 'Lucio and the lively Helena' (Act 1 Scene 2, lines 63–71); Mercutio's list of tragic ladies (Act 2 Scene 4, lines 34–8); and Juliet's account of all the things she would rather do than marry Paris:

> O bid me leap, rather than marry Paris,
> From off the battlements of any tower,
> Or walk in thievish ways, or bid me lurk
> Where serpents are; chain me with roaring bears
>
> *(Act 4 Scene 1, lines 77–85)*

One type of list which is characteristic of *Romeo and Juliet* is the blazon, a technique of romantic poetry that itemised and idealised the features of a loved one. Shakespeare seems to question or parody the technique at several points in the play, as in the following three examples. In the first, Juliet rejects what Romeo might be; in the second, Mercutio burlesques the convention; and in the third, the Nurse reverses the usual male praise of a female.

> What's Montague? It is nor hand nor foot,
> Nor arm nor face, nor any other part
> Belonging to a man.   *(Act 2 Scene 2, lines 40–2)*

> I conjure thee by Rosaline's bright eyes,
> By her high forehead and her scarlet lip,

By her fine foot, straight leg, and quivering thigh,
And the demesnes that there adjacent lie

(Act 2 Scene 1, lines 17–20)

... though his face be better than any man's, yet his leg excels
all men's, and for a hand and a foot and a body, though they
be not to be talked on, yet they are past compare.

(Act 2 Scene 5, lines 39–42)

Such lists provide valuable opportunities for actors to vary their delivery. In speaking, a character usually seeks to give each 'item' a distinctiveness in emphasis and emotional tone, and sometimes an accompanying action and expression. In addition, the accumulating effect of lists can add to the force of argument, enrich atmosphere, amplify meaning and provide extra dimensions of character.

Verse and prose

In Shakespeare's time, audiences expected actors in tragedies to speak in verse. The poetic style was thought to be particularly suitable for tragic themes and moments of high dramatic or emotional intensity. Another influence on the language of *Romeo and Juliet* is the popularity of sonnets at the time the play was written. The Chorus' two speeches and the lovers' first meeting are in 14-line sonnet form, and many other speeches show the influence of the sonnet tradition (see pages 56–8).

Although there is a good deal of rhyme, much of the language of *Romeo and Juliet* is blank verse: unrhymed verse written in iambic pentameter. It is conventional to define iambic pentameter as a rhythm or metre in which each line has five stressed syllables (/) alternating with five unstressed syllables (×):

   ×   /   ×   /   ×   /   ×   /   ×   /
   But soft, what light through yonder window breaks?

At school, Shakespeare had learned the technical definition of iambic pentameter. In Greek, *penta* means 'five', and *iamb* means a 'foot' of two syllables, the first unstressed, the second stressed (as in 'alas' = aLAS). Shakespeare practised writing in that metre, and his early plays, such as *Titus Andronicus* or *Richard III*, are very regular in rhythm (often expressed as de-DUM de-DUM de-DUM de-DUM de-DUM), and with each line 'end-stopped' (making sense on its own).

Romeo and Juliet is also a fairly 'early' play (*c.* 1595), but with the experience of having written almost a dozen plays, Shakespeare was becoming more flexible and experimental in his use of iambic pentameter. There is general critical agreement that a good deal of the play's verse achieves greater maturity of feeling than in earlier plays. The 'five-beat' rhythm is still often obvious, but at other times, notably in the 'balcony' scene, less prominent. End-stopped lines are less frequent. There is greater use of enjambement (running on), where one line flows on into the next, seemingly with little or no pause:

> O speak again, bright angel, for thou art
> As glorious to this night, being o'er my head,
> As is a wingèd messenger of heaven
> Unto the white-upturnèd wond'ring eyes
> Of mortals that fall back to gaze on him
>
> *(Act 2 Scene 2, lines 26–30)*

Some critics, directors and actors have strong convictions about how the verse should be spoken. For example, the director Peter Hall insists there should always be a pause at the end of each line. But it seems appropriate when studying (or watching, or acting in) *Romeo and Juliet,* not to attempt to apply rigid rules about how the verse should be spoken. Shakespeare certainly used the convention of iambic pentameter, but he did not adhere to it slavishly. He knew 'the rules', but he was not afraid to break them to suit his dramatic purpose. No one knows for sure just how the lines were delivered on Shakespeare's own stage, and today actors use their discretion in how to deliver the lines. They pause or emphasise words to convey meaning and emotion and to avoid the mechanical or clockwork-sounding speech that a too slavish attention to the pentameter line might produce.

About 88 per cent of the play is in verse, only 12 per cent is in prose. How did Shakespeare decide whether to write in verse or prose? One answer is that he followed theatrical convention. Prose was traditionally used by comic and low-status characters. High-status characters spoke verse. But in *Romeo and Juliet,* the Nurse (low-status) speaks a good deal of verse. That may be because of the context: when she is with high-status Lady Capulet and Juliet. Further, Romeo, Mercutio and Benvolio (all high-status) use prose in Act 2 Scene 4. Here, the reason may be because their talk is 'comic'. And notably, breaking the conventional rule that death scenes in tragedy should be in verse, Shakespeare has Mercutio, at the point of death, speak in prose (Act 3 Scene 1, lines 88–94).

Critical approaches

Traditional criticism

Romeo and Juliet has always been very popular on stage, but critics have tended to regard it as less profound and complex than the tragedies that Shakespeare wrote five to ten years later: *Hamlet*, *Othello*, *King Lear* and *Macbeth*. Although it has not received as much critical attention as those four plays, it is possible to detect certain trends in critical approaches to *Romeo and Juliet*. In 1765, Doctor Samuel Johnson, perhaps the greatest of the eighteenth-century critics, praised the play for its variety and appeal:

> The scenes are busy and various, the incidents numerous and important, the catastrophe irresistibly affecting

Later critics echoed Johnson's praise, and increasingly focused their attention on characters, often treating them as real persons. From the late eighteenth century, through the nineteenth, and well into the twentieth, criticism mainly centred on character. Nineteenth-century style often soared to romantic excess, as in Samuel Taylor Coleridge's comment in 1813:

> With Juliet love has all that is tender and melancholy in the nightingale, all that is voluptuous in the rose, with whatever is sweet in the freshness of spring; but it ends with a long deep sigh, like the breeze of the evening.

The same romantic floweriness is evident in William Hazlitt's significantly titled *The Characters of Shakespeare's Plays* (1817): 'the heart beats, the blood circulates and mantles throughout'. But Hazlitt perceptively observes that Shakespeare

> founded the passion of the two lovers not on the pleasures they had experienced, but on all the pleasures they had not experienced.

Coleridge and Hazlitt, in their romantic concern for character, effectively set the tone for nineteenth-century criticism of the play. But the critic with whom the expression 'character study' is most associated is A C Bradley. Around 100 years ago, Bradley delivered a course of lectures at Oxford University which were published in 1904 as *Shakespearean Tragedy*. The book has never been out of print, and Bradley's approach has been hugely influential. Although Bradley only briefly discusses *Romeo and Juliet* (he is centrally concerned with *Hamlet, Macbeth, Othello, King Lear*) labelling it as an 'immature' tragedy, his form of criticism reflects previous approaches to the play, and has strongly influenced critical approaches right up to the present day.

Bradley talks of the characters in Shakespeare as if they were real human beings existing in worlds recognisable to modern readers. He identifies the unique desires and motives which give characters their particular personalities, and which evoke feelings of admiration or disapproval in the audience. Assuming that each character experiences familiar human emotions and thoughts, Bradley's presentation of conflict in Shakespeare's tragedies is primarily that within the individual – an inward struggle. Following Aristotle's theory that a tragic hero has a fatal flaw, Bradley sees each hero in Shakespeare's tragedies struggling with circumstances and fate, and afflicted with a personal defect which causes the tragedy:

> a marked one-sidedness, a predisposition in some particular direction; a total incapacity, in certain circumstances, of resisting the force which draws in this direction; a fatal tendency to identify the whole being with one interest, object, passion or habit of mind. This, it would seem, is, for Shakespeare, the fundamental tragic trait . . . some marked imperfection or defect: irresolution, precipitancy, pride, credulousness, excessive simplicity, excessive susceptibility to sexual emotions and the like . . . these contribute decisively to the conflict and catastrophe.

Bradley's character approach has been much criticised. For example, it is evident that most of Shakespeare's tragic characters possess more than 'one interest, object, passion or habit of mind'. Romeo's revengeful killing of Tybalt shows that he is not motivated only by what Bradley calls 'excessive susceptibility to sexual emotions'.

A second criticism is that a focus on character neglects the Elizabethan contexts of the play's creation: the cultural and intellectual assumptions of the time, stage conditions, and poetic and dramatic conventions. The section on Contexts in this Guide demonstrates the powerful influence on *Romeo and Juliet* of such contexts.

Third, Bradley's view of tragedy as a mysterious process which somehow restores order and harmony has been condemned as an obscure metaphysical assumption. Much modern criticism rejects interpretations which assert that the play ends unambiguously in reconciliation and peace. It does not accept that the death of the lovers is a sacrifice which atones for the sins of the Montagues and Capulets and ends their feud. In the same vein, modern criticism is also sceptical of Bradley's argument that 'fate' plays a large part in tragedy. That view, which derives from the tragedies of classical Greece, diverts attention away from a critical search for the social causes of the tragedy of Romeo and Juliet.

The most frequent objection to Bradley is his treatment of characters as real people. Modern criticism is uneasy about discussing characters in this way, preferring to see them as fictional creations in a stage drama. But although Bradley has fallen from critical favour, his influence is still evident. As pages 118–123 show, it is difficult to avoid talking or writing about characters as if they were living people and making moral judgements on them. The notion of a tragic flaw has proved similarly powerful. Interpretations continue to locate the cause of the tragedy in the lovers' 'precipitancy' (to use Bradley's word): the impetuous rashness of both Romeo and Juliet.

Following Bradley, and sharing his assumptions, Caroline Spurgeon opened up a fresh perspective on *Romeo and Juliet*: the study of its imagery. In her book *Shakespeare's Imagery and What it Tells Us*, Spurgeon counted over 200 images in the play. She analysed them into different groups according to their subject matter, for example images from nature, animals, food and cooking, war and weapons and so on. Recurring image clusters, or 'iterative imagery', help create atmosphere and embody and express the preoccupations of the play (see page 75). Spurgeon was particularly attracted to the images of light in *Romeo and Juliet*:

> ... the beauty and ardour of young love are seen by
> Shakespeare as the irradiating glory of sunlight and starlight in

a dark world. The dominating image is *light*, every form and manifestation of it: the sun, moon, stars, fire, lightning, the flash of gunpowder, and the reflected life of beauty and of love; while by contrast we have night, darkness, clouds, rain, mist and smoke. Each of the lovers thinks of the other as light ... To Juliet, Romeo is 'day in night'; to Romeo, Juliet is the sun rising from the east, and when they soar to love's ecstasy, each alike pictures the other as stars in heaven, shedding such brightness as puts to shame the heavenly bodies themselves ... Shakespeare saw the story, in its swift and tragic beauty, as an almost blinding flash of light, suddenly ignited, and as swiftly quenched

The value of Caroline Spurgeon's pioneering study of Shakespeare's imagery has been acknowledged by later critics, but her work has also been much criticised. She entirely overlooks the many sexual images in *Romeo and Juliet*, and rarely examines how the imagery relates to the dramatic context or contributes to the oppositions that characterise the play. She claims that characters' opinions are Shakespeare's own, and that the imagery reveals his personality (for example, that he has 'sympathy for snails'). A further criticism is that Spurgeon's tone is invariably one of praise, avoiding any negative appraisal of the play's imagery (echoing the 'bardolatry' that has dogged Shakespeare criticism ever since the Romantics of the early nineteenth century). Other critics have been more sceptical, arguing that because Shakespeare wrote the play fairly early in his career he sometimes uses excessively elaborate imagery or 'conceits' (see page 76).

Other critics have followed Spurgeon's example in paying detailed attention to the language of the play. Wolfgang Clemen further developed her finding that repeated image clusters help establish the themes or leitmotifs of the play. M M Mahood's study of wordplay reveals the sheer amount of punning in *Romeo and Juliet*. She estimates that there are 175 such 'quibbles', beginning with the pun on 'colliers', 'choler', and 'collar' that opens the play. Mahood identifies how such wordplay is dramatically functional in patterning the imagery, giving outlet to characters' feelings, and sharpening dramatic irony. Her many examples include: the sexual punning throughout the play; the images of Death as Juliet's bridegroom (see page 77); Romeo's quibbles on love as a sickness, slavery and conquest; the punning matches between Mercutio and Romeo; and the grim joke in Mercutio's dying pun, 'Ask for me tomorrow and you shall find me a grave man.'

Harold Bloom is the most recent critic to write in the tradition of Bradley's character criticism. In *Shakespeare: The Invention of the Human*, Bloom argues that Shakespeare's characters provided the self-reflexive models by which human beings first acquired selves to reflect on (or, to put it more simply, Shakespeare's characters first showed us how to think about ourselves). That enormous claim about the origin of our subjectivity is disputed by almost all scholars, many of whom are dismissive of Bloom's character study approach as gushing and exaggerated.

Some of Bloom's judgements are surprising. He declares that both Mercutio and the Nurse are 'inwardly cold', and that in the Nurse's tale of Juliet's childhood 'we do not hear the accents of love'. Bloom would be on safer ground writing 'I' rather than 'we' in that comment. But Bloom's interpretations can provoke valuable argument and he does acknowledge, without any further elaboration but with an elaborate rhetorical flourish, that the lovers are caught in a complex web of powerful influences:

> everything is against the lovers – their families and the state, the indifference of nature, the vagaries of time, and the regressive movement of the cosmological contraries of love and strife

Bloom's book was published in 1999, and he opens his discussion of *Romeo and Juliet* with a jaundiced comment on other critics of the play. His remark gives a clue to recent changes in critical writing:

> Alas . . . the tragedy is more frequently surrendered to commissars of gender and power, who can thrash the patriarchy, including Shakespeare himself, for victimising Juliet.

Bloom obviously disapproves of critics who approach *Romeo and Juliet* from the standpoint of feminism or politics. But these and other modern approaches have expanded understanding of the play beyond traditional criticism of character and language. The following sections show how, increasingly throughout the second half of the twentieth century and in the twenty-first, critical approaches to Shakespeare have radically challenged the traditional approaches described above.

Modern criticism

Modern criticism argues that traditional approaches to *Romeo and Juliet*, with their focus on character, are too individualistic. The concentration on personal feelings ignores society and history, and so divorces literary, dramatic and aesthetic matters from their social context. Contemporary critical perspectives therefore shift the focus from individuals to how social conditions of Verona (and Elizabethan England) are reflected in characters' relationships, language and behaviour. Modern criticism also concerns itself with how changing social assumptions at different periods of time have affected both literary and theatrical interpretations of the play.

Before examining particular examples of recent critical approaches to *Romeo and Juliet*, it is helpful to summarise the major features that such perspectives commonly share. Contemporary Shakespeare criticism:

- is sceptical of 'character' approaches (but often uses them – see pages 118–123);
- concentrates on political, social and economic factors (arguing that these factors determine Shakespeare's creativity and audiences' and critics' interpretations);
- plays down or rejects supernatural and mysterious explanations (such as 'fate', 'the stars' or 'fortune');
- identifies contradictions, fragmentation and disunity in the plays;
- questions the possibility of 'happy' or 'hopeful' endings, preferring ambiguous, unsettling or sombre endings (the feud is not resolved);
- produces readings that are subversive of existing social structures;
- identifies how the plays express the interests of dominant groups, particularly rich and powerful males;
- insists that 'theory' (psychological, social, etc.) is essential to produce valid readings;
- often expresses its commitment (for example, to feminism, or equality, or political change);

- argues that all readings are political or ideological readings (and that traditional criticism falsely claims to be objective);
- argues that traditional approaches have always interpreted Shakespeare conservatively, in ways that confirm and maintain the interests of the elite or dominant class.

Political criticism

'Political criticism' is a convenient label for approaches concerned with power and social structure. Such approaches to *Romeo and Juliet* are less concerned with love than with how factions tighten their grip on wealth, power and status in Verona. They argue that the tragedy springs from the condition of society itself. Romeo and Juliet's personal plight must be understood in the context of the political world of the play: its social structure and its feuding families. It is a world where the values of property and commerce challenge those of love and friendship. Such interpretations highlight the contrast between the great feasts at Capulet's house and the poverty of the Apothecary. They see Shakespeare making a social criticism in that contrast and in Romeo's condemnation of the corrupting power of gold:

> There is thy gold, worse poison to men's souls,
> Doing more murder in this loathsome world,
> Than these poor compounds that thou mayst not sell.
> I sell thee poison, thou hast sold me none.
>
> *(Act 5 Scene 1, lines 80–3)*

In an essay written to accompany a production at London's Young Vic theatre, the critic Richard Wilson sees Verona as a tense urban space, an aggressively competitive city. He views Capulet and Montague as warring mafia godfathers (as they are portrayed in Baz Luhrmann's film). Wilson asserts that Prince Escales' name is highly symbolic of Verona's values, because 'Escales' means 'ladder', and the Prince is at the top of that ladder. Other critics see Escales' position as far from secure. For example, Dympna Callaghan interprets the play as a power struggle between family, church and state, with Escales struggling for control over his rebellious subjects in his three appearances in the play.

Wilson and other political critics argue that Montague and Capulet compete at the end of the play as to who can erect the largest and most expensive statue of their dead children. This interpretation illustrates the occasionally close relationship between a stage production and academic criticism. For example, Michael Bogdanov's 1986 production for the Royal Shakespeare Company ended with Juliet's death. The stage then transformed into a publicity stunt performed before television and press cameras. Golden statues of the dead lovers were unveiled and Montague and Capulet posed for the cameras. This staging reflects academic criticism which argues that when the two fathers say they will raise the lovers' statues in pure gold they are displaying the materialistic values that poison social relationships in Verona.

Many productions in the second half of the twentieth century have attempted to find political significance in the play through their presentation of the feuding families. Just as 'Romeo and Juliet' has long been used in newspaper headlines to describe any cross-community love affair, so the lovers' opposing backgrounds have been portrayed vividly on stage: Jew versus Arab, Protestant versus Catholic, Serb versus Croat, black versus white. But some critics argue that productions which present such starkly opposed 'families' mistake the political and ethnic nature of Shakespeare's setting. As the Prologue and the whole play make clear, the Montagues and Capulets share the same culture. Their ethnicity, religion, status, language, politics, beliefs and social practices are identical. They truly are:

Two households, both alike in dignity   *(Prologue line 1)*

Verona is a divided city, but its factions belong within the same community. Neither the Montagues nor the Capulets are 'outsiders', and each has equal claim to high status. Interestingly, the films of Zeffirelli and Luhrmann both emphasise how alike the two families really are. Although the Luhrmann film dresses the young men of the two households differently (beachwear versus black leather) it is evident that they are similar mafia families, divided only by hate for each other.

Critics have used that similarity to demonstrate how Shakespeare heightens the dramatic intensity of the feud by having the two families set in the same cultural community. For example, Susan Snyder uses the concept of ideology to argue that nothing divides the Montagues and Capulets but their names. In all other respects they are virtually indistinguishable. In this way, the feud becomes ideology, a belief that pervades every aspect of Verona. Names alone define what each person is, and that arbitrary 'placing' of each individual in their social role gives added poignancy and urgency to Juliet's questions and commands:

> O Romeo, Romeo, wherefore art thou Romeo?
> Deny thy father and refuse thy name;
> Or if thou wilt not, be but sworn my love,
> And I'll no longer be a Capulet
>
> . . .
>
> 'Tis but thy name that is my enemy;
> Thou art thyself, though not a Montague.
> What's Montague? It is nor hand nor foot,
> Nor arm nor face, nor any other part
> Belonging to a man. O be some other name!
> What's in a name?   *(Act 2 Scene 2, lines 33–43)*

Shakespeare thus invites the audience to realise that in the hate-ridden culture of Verona the answer to 'What's in a name?' is 'Everything!' The feud is artificial and irrational, because nothing more than a name is the basis of each individual's identity. Names are at the root of the conflict that corrupts Verona, setting neighbour against neighbour. Every character is affected by the feud of the two families. As soon as a person knows the name of another, the emotional mood changes, as Juliet's reaction demonstrates so vividly:

NURSE   His name is Romeo, and a Montague,
         The only son of your great enemy.
JULIET   My only love sprung from my only hate!

                                    (Act 1 Scene 5, lines 135–7)

Snyder argues that the ideology of the feud (which is little more than the belief that if a character's name is Montague then he or she is your enemy) constructs the social world of Verona. Romeo later expresses his recognition of the poisonous effect of names in Verona when he asks 'In what vile part of this anatomy / Doth my name lodge?' (Act 3 Scene 3, lines 106–7) and threatens to cut out that part with his dagger. Looking at the play in this way is to see it as the tragic failure of two young people who cannot break free of their constraining social world and be themselves. Neither can fulfil Juliet's command to 'Deny thy father and refuse thy name'.

Feminist criticism

Feminism aims to achieve rights and equality for women in social, political and economic life. It challenges sexism: those beliefs and practices which result in the degradation, oppression and subordination of one sex over the other. Feminist critics therefore reject 'male ownership' of criticism in which men determined what questions were to be asked of a play, and which answers were acceptable. They argue that male criticism often neglects, represses or misrepresents female experience, and stereotypes or distorts the woman's point of view.

Feminist criticism, like any 'approach', takes a wide variety of forms. Nonetheless it is possible to identify certain major concerns for feminist critical writing on *Romeo and Juliet*: the exposure of patriarchy, the rejection of the idealisation of romantic love, male bonding, male anxiety, and women's resistance of patriarchy.

Most commonly, feminists approach the play using the notion of patriarchy (male domination of women). They see issues of power and control as crucial to understanding the play. Feminists point to the fact that throughout much of history power has been in the hands of men, both in society and in the family. *Romeo and Juliet* clearly reflects that male domination of women, particularly in how Capulet rules his household, his wife and his daughter. His treatment of Juliet is central to feminist criticism in exposing patriarchy as vicious and unjust.

Capulet regards his daughter as a male possession, like the other property he owns. He feels free to dispose of her however he wishes ('And you be mine, I'll give you to my friend'). She is a bargaining chip in negotiations to ally his family to that of the Prince (Paris is the Prince's kinsman). Like many other fathers in Shakespeare's plays, Capulet is enraged when his daughter disobeys him. He humiliates and insults her ('green-sickness carrion', 'baggage', 'tallow-face', 'whining mammet') and theatens her with violence ('My fingers itch'). He warns Juliet what will happen if she continues her disobedience:

hang, beg, starve, die in the streets   *(Act 3 Scene 5, line 192)*

For feminists, the feud illustrates the extreme form of patriarchal society. It symbolises the malevolent masculinity that pervades Verona. Gangs of young men clash in pursuit of the enmity of their masters. The opening of the play, with its crude sexual joking, is evidence of the city's macho male culture. Sampson and Gregory see sex as violence against women, used to express male dominance. To be a man means to rape and to kill rivals. But in its exposure of the patriarchal assumptions embodied in the play, feminist critics draw attention to other episodes and language that are often overlooked or played down by many male critics. Examples include:

- The Nurse's tale of how her husband laughed at the two-year-old Juliet tumbling over ('Thou wilt fall backward when thou hast more wit') suggests that as a child Juliet was subjected to coarse masculine teasing.
- Mercutio's mocking conjuration of Romeo outside Capulet's orchard is a blazon (a list, see page 80) which reduces a woman simply to the physical parts which men find sexually attractive:

> I conjure thee by Rosaline's bright eyes,
> By her high forehead and her scarlet lip,
> By her fine foot, straight leg, and quivering thigh,
> And the demesnes that there adjacent lie
>
> *(Act 2 Scene 1, lines 17–20)*

- The Nurse's harassment by Mercutio in Act 2 Scene 4 ('A bawd, a bawd, a bawd!') is often interpreted, and played on stage, as good-humoured teasing. But it reveals more of the male bullying that pervades Verona.
- Capulet's bullying language treats Juliet as little more than a farmyard animal ('fettle your fine joints', 'Graze where you will').
- Capulet's grief expressed over the 'dead' Juliet contrasts with that of his wife. She mourns the death of 'one poor and loving child'. His language regrets his loss of inheritance:

> Death is my son-in-law, Death is my heir,
> My daughter he hath wedded. I will die,
> And leave him all; life, living, all is Death's.
>
> *(Act 4 Scene 5, lines 38–40)*

- Capulet's good humour, and his apparent concern in Act 1 Scene 2 for Juliet to have a choice in who she marries, only serves to heighten the capricious nature of patriarchy. His true feelings are revealed when Juliet defies his choice of husband for her.

Such readings (like all critical interpretations) raise the question of whether they are what Shakespeare intended. Whilst many critics today argue that Shakespeare's intentions can never be known (and that any play can carry meanings that are not 'intended'), Susan Bassnett is confident that in the final scene when Montague and Capulet agree to set up golden statues of their children

> Shakespeare wanted to stress the vulgarity of the two fathers and depict them in a less than sympathetic light.

Feminist criticism also draws attention to the male bonding that characterises the play. Like much traditional criticism, feminism identifies Tybalt's language and behaviour as revealing the extreme nature of the masculine codes of honour which drive the young males of the play. But feminism also sees the male friendships of the play as partly responsible for the tragedy. Male friendship results in Mercutio defending Romeo and losing his life for him, followed by the fight to the death as Romeo avenges his friend Mercutio. Feminist criticism sees in this a crucial expression of the conflict between love for a wife versus love for a male friend.

Feminism also differs from traditional criticism in its interpretation of the way that Mercutio, Romeo and Benvolio joke together. Feminists detect a malign undercurrent to this male sociability. In Act 2 Scene 4, Romeo, joyful at the prospect of marrying Juliet, meets his two friends and engages in what criticism has conventionally described as witty wordplay. Mercutio, delighted, exclaims 'Now art thou sociable, now art thou Romeo' (lines 72–3). Feminists have interpreted this as signifying the underlying macho culture of Verona: it is only when men join together in sexual joking that they think they are truly themselves. In such an interpretation, it is male friendship rather than love that is the driving force of the play, because love is reduced to the crudity of Mercutio's view:

> this drivelling love is like a great natural that runs lolling up
> and down to hide his bauble in a hole.
>
> *(Act 2 Scene 4, lines 74–5)*

Mercutio's inability to reconcile tender affection with sexual desire is a major reason why feminist critics reject the conventional critical view of the play which sees it as crucially about romantic love. Both Mercutio and the Nurse continually stress the physical aspects of sex. Their repeated equation of love with sex undermines the idealisation of love that some traditional criticism has claimed is the essence of the play (see the quotations from Samuel Taylor Coleridge and Hazlitt, page 84).

Feminist interpretations also suggest that male anxiety is evident throughout the play as men feel their mastery challenged. Capulet demands of Tybalt 'Am I the master here or you?' This is the familiar expression of any dominant male asserting his mastery over a young challenger. But there are deeper concerns. Losing one's manhood, or behaving like a woman are evident fears. Feminists detect male disquiet about virility behind Capulet's rebuke of Tybalt ('goodman boy', 'you'll be the man!' 'You are a saucy boy'). They see that male anxiety about manhood intensified when Tybalt turns the accusation on to Romeo, calling him 'Boy' and 'wretched boy'.

Feminists detect Shakespeare giving further powerful expression to male anxiety about loss of manhood as Romeo exclaims 'Juliet, / Thy beauty hath made me effeminate', and when Friar Lawrence upbraids him: 'Art thou a man? . . . thy tears are womanish'. Such comments arise from the male assumption that women are weak and men are masterful. That assumption is also undermined, claim feminist critics, as the play reveals men losing mastery of their own emotions. Romeo cries like Juliet, 'blubbering and weeping' at the thought of banishment. Capulet loses control as he rages against Juliet. In the tomb, Friar Lawrence panics and abandons Juliet.

The most obvious source of male anxiety is the female challenge to men's power. That is most evident when Juliet refuses to obey her father's wish that she marry Paris. Her defiance, and her consequent deception of her parents, exemplifies female resistance in a male world. Juliet's bravery as she willingly risks death is a clear example of the limits of patriarchy: the 13-year-old girl retains some control over her life, even if it is only in the power to end it.

Feminists detect other examples of female dissent from male power. They detect some hints of female solidarity as both Lady Capulet and the Nurse protest against Capulet's harsh treatment of Juliet. Lady Capulet resists male authority in other ways. Her first words in the play mock her husband: 'A crutch, a crutch! why call you for a sword?'. Her words may be a comment on his lack of sexual potency. In the preparations for the wedding feast she seems to respond with spirit, as if she suspects him of affairs with other women: 'But I will watch you from such watching now'. Such examples lead Sasha Roberts to conclude that 'the play portrays a crisis in patriarchal authority'.

Lady Capulet seems very much younger than her husband. Feminists argue that Capulet dominates his wife as he dominates his daughter. Their relationship is far from a partnership, and may be one of domestic violence. That interpretation of Lady Capulet as victim of her husband's power and as a woman who therefore retreats into her own private world is sometimes justified by pointing to how she reacts to Juliet's evident distress. Lady Capulet makes no effort to understand just why Juliet reacts so strongly to the prospect of marriage. She simply washes her hands of the matter, leaving it to her husband: 'Tell him so yourself'. As Capulet explodes into rage, Lady Capulet can do little to protect Juliet. She finally rejects her daughter:

> Talk not to me, for I'll not speak a word.
> Do as thou wilt, for I have done with thee.
>
> *(Act 3 Scene 5, lines 202–3)*

Performance criticism

Performance criticism fully acknowledges that *Romeo and Juliet* is a play: a script to be performed by actors to an audience. It examines all aspects of the play in performance: its staging in the theatre or on film and video. Performance criticism focuses on Shakespeare's stagecraft and the semiotics of theatre (signs: words, costumes, gestures, etc.), together with the 'afterlife' of the play (what happened to *Romeo and Juliet* after Shakespeare wrote it). That involves scrutiny of how productions at different periods have presented the play. As such, performance criticism appraises how the text has been cut, added to, rewritten and rearranged to present a version felt appropriate to the times.

A study of *Romeo and Juliet*'s afterlife also shows how the play has been the inspiration for all kinds of 'offshoots' or adaptations. These include music, operas, ballets, paintings, cartoons, advertisements, films, and all kinds of prose and verse stories. Many lampoons and parodies exist, especially of the 'balcony' scene. *Romeo and Juliet*'s capacity to create an infinity of meanings is evident in its huge cultural legacy. Aspects of the play appear in all areas of 'popular' and 'high' culture.

Performance criticism vividly reveals the instability of *Romeo and Juliet*. The play takes very different forms in its afterlife, performed and received very differently at different times. The instability begins with the existence of three versions of the play, the First and Second Quartos and the Folio (see pages 52–3). It is heightened by the way in which directors and actors have created new performances of the play over the centuries.

The play has always been a star vehicle for the major actors of each generation. But in every age the text has been significantly amended. For over 400 years since its first performance, some time around 1595, audiences have watched and heard very different versions. The following brief description of some of those versions shows there is no such thing as the 'authentic' *Romeo and Juliet*.

In Shakespeare's time, Juliet was played by a boy. This may have added to the appeal of the play, perhaps bringing to it a dangerous implication of homoeroticism. It was an age when homosexuality could be punished by death, and yet audiences watched two boys (Juliet and Romeo) kissing in public. Although there is no record of an actual performance before 1660, many references testify to the play's popularity. It seems that, with the exception of the 18-year period when all theatres were closed under the Commonwealth (1642–60), *Romeo and Juliet* has never been absent for long from the stage. But not everyone enjoyed it. In 1662, Samuel Pepys saw the play and wrote in his diary 'it is of itself the worst that ever I heard in my life'.

Pepys' low opinion may well have been echoed by his contemporaries because, although the play continued to be performed, it seems to have been thought in need of improvement to make it more acceptable to contemporary tastes. Shakespeare's play was therefore substantially rewritten in 1680 by Thomas Otway and given a new title, *The History and Fall of Caius Marius*. It included such lines as 'O Marius, Marius! Wherefore art thou Marius?' This version, set in classical Rome, was held to be more refined than Shakespeare's.

Otway's adaptation was the version performed until 1748, when the famous actor-manager David Garrick wrote his own version.

Garrick wanted to clear Shakespeare's play of what he called 'jingle and quibble', and to make the play suitable for a respectable eighteenth-century audience. He retained much of Otway's version, raised Juliet's age to 18 (see page 65), cut the many sexual references ('bawdy quibbles'), and added a funeral procession in which the Capulets took Juliet to the tomb. Garrick removed all reference to Romeo's love for Rosaline, and followed Otway in having Juliet wake and talk with Romeo before they both die. An extract from Garrick's invented scene gives a flavour of its quality:

JULIET   And did I wake for this?
ROMEO   My powers are blasted.
    'Twixt death and love I'm torn, I am distracted!
    But death's strongest – and I must leave thee, Juliet!
    Oh cruel, cursed fate! in sight of heaven!
JULIET   Thou ravest; lean on my breast.
ROMEO   Fathers have flinty hearts, no tears can melt 'em.
    Nature pleads in vain. Children must be wretched.
JULIET   O! My breaking heart!
ROMEO   She is my wife; our hearts are twined together.
    Capulet forbear! Paris loose your hold!
    Pull not our heartstrings thus; they crack, they break.
    O! Juliet! Juliet! (*Dies*)

Today, these lines are regarded as comic, and Garrick's whole adaptation is judged as sentimental and sanitised. But it was much admired in its time and was the version performed on stage for almost 100 years. It was not until 1845 that the Garrick version was rejected. Interestingly, there was a vogue at the time for females playing Romeo, and it was an American actress, Charlotte Cushman, who effectively restored Shakespeare's version to the stage (but in a heavily cut form, with all the sexual joking omitted).

The nineteenth century saw many spectacular productions which presented a romantic interpretation. Elaborate scenery and costumes, full of period detail, attempted to create an illusion of an historically 'authentic' Verona (which in practice meant a Victorian conception of Renaissance Italy).

The twentieth century saw a return to much simpler stagings. Productions no longer attempted to create an impression of realism. Under the influence of William Poel and Harley Granville Barker, the stage was cleared of the clutter of historical detail. The aim was to recapture the conditions of the Elizabethan bare stage which was not dependent on theatrical illusion. That implied a minimum of scenery, scenes flowing swiftly into each other, and a concern for clear speaking of Shakespeare's language. You can find a valuable account of such staging conditions in Gurr and Ichikawa, *Staging in Shakespeare's Theatres*. Granville Barker, himself a playwright and director, was an early and influential writer of performance criticism. His *Prefaces to Shakespeare* conducts the reader through *Romeo and Juliet* giving prescriptive advice on staging and characterisation.

There has been huge variation in how the play has been performed over the past 100 years. But it is generally true to say that productions have moved away from very romantic portrayals of the lovers to those which set their love in the context of the underlying brutality of Verona. That is, a shift to productions which are concerned with exposing the unpleasant social aspects of the play. Two examples have become well-known (or notorious). Michael Bogdanov's 1986 production staged the ending as a cynical media stunt (see page 50). Karen Beier's 1995 German production, set in a concrete shell, ended in spiritual desolation: Romeo tried vainly to retch up the poison, and Friar Lawrence gabbled his long story to the audience, making it sound like a series of frantic excuses in an attempt to escape any blame.

Such productions are a reminder of a question about *Romeo and Juliet* that has long puzzled critics: what kind of play is it? The two endings just described do not result in catharsis (purging the emotions through pity and fear), which Aristotle argued to be a necessary feature of tragedy. Similarly, as noted on page 59, the play's two main characters are young and powerless, quite unlike the traditional heroes of tragedy, kings or great warriors. There is a good deal of comedy in the play, especially up to the death of Mercutio. Yet both Quarto versions of the play, published in 1597 and 1599, describe it in their titles as a tragedy, and in the 1623 Folio which divides the plays into Histories, Comedies and Tragedies, *Romeo and Juliet* is placed in the Tragedies.

Concerns about genre (type of play) began very early. In 1621, the writer Robert Burton (see page 54) described *Romeo and Juliet* as a 'tragicomedy of love' and, ever since, critics have invented numerous genre descriptions:

- a 'tragedy of character' (the disaster is caused by the recklessness of the two young lovers – their 'tragic flaw')
- a 'tragedy of fate' (the lovers are 'star-crossed', and 'death-marked' – the lovers are the victims of the malign influence of fate)
- a 'tragedy of state' (Romeo and Juliet are victims of society)
- a 'romantic tragedy' (love and tragedy are mutually linked)

H B Charlton's view is that the play is a 'failed tragedy'. He argues that it is an 'unsuccessful experiment' by Shakespeare who was still learning his trade as a playwright. But it seems likely that arguments about genre will persist. Stanley Wells, one of the leading practitioners of performance criticism, considers the way the play has been criticised and altered over the centuries and concludes:

> perhaps the play's greatest challenge is to our notions of genre. The script can be interpreted in all its richness and diversity only if we abandon the idea that because it is called a tragedy it must centre on the fate of individuals, and accept its emphasis on the multifarious society in which these individuals have their being.

Psychoanalytic criticism

In the twentieth century, psychoanalysis became a major influence on the understanding and interpretation of human behaviour. The founder of psychoanalysis, Sigmund Freud, explained personality as the result of unconscious and irrational desires, repressed memories or wishes, sexuality, fantasy, anxiety and conflict. Freud's theories have had a strong influence on criticism and stagings of Shakespeare's plays, most obviously on *Hamlet* in the well-known claim that Hamlet suffers from an Oedipus complex.

An example of a psychoanalytic approach to *Romeo and Juliet* might use the notion of unconscious desire (motivations of which the individual is not aware). It claims that a death wish lies behind the excessively masculine culture of Verona, arguing that male violence instinctively seeks death for the men who exercise it. It also sees that death wish inherent in love itself, expressed in the play's use of the word 'die' (which for Elizabethans could also mean sexual orgasm). One psychoanalytic interpretation has even suggested that when Juliet kills herself she is in effect making love to Romeo's dagger.

Because psychoanalysis is concerned with dreams, and with personal trauma or anxiety, Mercutio's freewheeling imagination has held particular appeal. Psychoanalytic critics see great significance in his Queen Mab speech, with its rapidly changing dream-like images and its erotic climax. Feminists draw on the assumptions of psychoanalysis in seeing the speech as expressing a male phobia: a fascinated fear of the female maternal body. For example, Sasha Roberts argues that Mercutio's use of the word 'hag'

> sounds a note of revulsion: women's conception and
> pregnancy become part of a nightmarish vision for Mercutio.

All these interpretations reveal the obvious weaknesses in applying psychoanalytic theories to *Romeo and Juliet*. Such theories cannot be proved or disproved, and they neglect historical and social factors. Psychoanalytic approaches are therefore often accused of imposing interpretations based on theory rather than upon Shakespeare's text. Nonetheless, their influence is evident in some productions. The films of Zeffirelli and Luhrmann both emphasise Mercutio's emotional disturbance, showing him behaving wildly, close to frenzy. Some stage productions have emphasised Mercutio's sexual anxiety. For example he has been portrayed as harbouring sexual desire for Romeo, and as an extreme case of misogyny (hatred of women). In a 1973 Royal Shakespeare Company production, Mercutio carried a life-size female doll, on to which he projected his disturbed feelings. He systematically tore it apart as he spoke the Queen Mab speech.

Postmodern criticism

Postmodern criticism (sometimes called 'deconstruction') is not always easy to understand because it is not centrally concerned with consistency or reasoned argument. It does not accept that one section of the story is necessarily connected to what follows, or that characters relate to each other in meaningful ways. Because of such assumptions, postmodern criticism is sometimes described as 'reading against the grain' or less politely as 'textual harassment'. The approach therefore has obvious drawbacks in providing a model for examination students who are expected to display reasoned, coherent argument, and respect for the evidence of the text.

Postmodern approaches to *Romeo and Juliet* are most clearly seen in stage productions. There, you could think of it as simply 'a mixture of styles'. The label 'postmodern' is applied to productions which selfconsciously show little regard for consistency in character, or for coherence in telling the story. Characters are dressed in costumes from very different historical periods, and carry both modern and ancient weapons. Ironically, Shakespeare himself has been regarded as a postmodern writer in the way he mixes genres in his plays, comedy with tragedy.

Postmodernism often revels in the cleverness of its own use of language, and accepts all kinds of anomalies and contradictions in a spirit of playfulness or 'carnival'. It abandons any notion of the organic unity of the play, and rejects the assumption that *Romeo and Juliet* possesses clear patterns or themes. Some postmodern critics even deny the possibility of finding meaning in language. They claim that words simply refer to other words, and so any interpretation is endlessly delayed (or 'deferred' as the deconstructionists say). Other critics focus on minor or marginal characters, or on gaps or silences in the play. They claim that these features, previously overlooked as unimportant, reveal significant truths about the play.

Baz Luhrmann's film *William Shakespeare's Romeo + Juliet* is a favourite subject for postmodern critics. For example, Carol Chillington Rutter argues that the film parodies both Shakespeare and Hollywood movies in its 'dazzling manipulation of film technology that simultaneously constructs and deconstructs the story'. She describes the film's setting, Verona Beach, as 'a postmodern cityscape'. It has a broken-down bandstand, 'Sycamore Grove' and a pool hall called 'The Globe'. The language is spoken 'like some crazy gangster rap', and in Rutter's view the women in the film 'register postmodern fragmentation' as Juliet's mother appears first as 'a gaping lipsticked mouth; the Nurse presents a screen-filling bottom . . . Juliet, a face and eyes'.

Luhrmann's MTV style and images from popular culture add to the deconstructive effect. Christian symbols appear throughout the film, but many are simply designer ornaments, fashionable items in a superficial society of conspicuous consumption, but empty of their religious meaning. Luhrmann creates a pastiche reality of this modern violent world by use of photographs, newspapers and film footage. The tragedy is announced on television news, and the film ends with a bleak image of a flickering television screen. In the words of the critic Patricia Tatspaugh, the device

> far from immortalising the young lovers, gives them nothing more than their fifteen minutes of fame, teenage suicides in a sensational crime story.

Organising your responses

The purpose of this chapter is to help you improve your writing about *Romeo and Juliet*. It offers practical guidance on two kinds of tasks: writing about an extract from the play and writing an essay. Whether you are answering an examination question, preparing coursework (term papers), or carrying out research into your own chosen topic, this section will help you organise and present your responses.

In all your writing, there are three vital things to remember:

- *Romeo and Juliet* is a play. Although it is usually referred to as a 'text', *Romeo and Juliet* is not a book, but a script intended to be acted on a stage. So, your writing should demonstrate an awareness of the play in performance as theatre. That means you should always try to read the play with an 'inner eye', thinking about how it could look and sound on stage. The next best thing to seeing an actual production is to imagine yourself sitting in the audience, watching and listening to *Romeo and Juliet* being performed. By doing so, you will be able to write effectively about Shakespeare's language and dramatic techniques.
- *Romeo and Juliet* is not a presentation of 'reality'. It is a dramatic construct in which the playwright, through theatre, engages the emotions and intellect of the audience. The characters and story may persuade an audience to suspend its disbelief for several hours. The audience may identify with the characters, be deeply moved by them, and may think of them as if they were living human beings. However, when you write, a major part of your task is to show how Shakespeare achieves his dramatic effects that so engage the audience. Through discussion of his handling of language, character and plot, your writing reveals how Shakespeare uses themes and ideas, attitudes and values, to give insight into crucial social, moral and political dilemmas of his time – and yours.
- How Shakespeare learned his craft. As a schoolboy, and in his early years as a dramatist, Shakespeare used all kinds of models or frameworks to guide his writing. But he quickly learned how to vary and adapt the models to his own dramatic purposes. Thi section offers frameworks that you can use to structure y

writing. As you use them, follow Shakespeare's example! Adapt them to suit your own writing style and needs.

Writing about an extract

It is an expected part of all Shakespeare study that you should be able to write well about an extract (sometimes called a 'passage') from the play. An extract is usually between 30 and 70 lines long, and you are invited to comment on it. The instructions vary. Sometimes the task is very briefly expressed:

- Write a detailed commentary on the following passage.
- Write about the effect of the extract on your own thoughts and feelings.

At other times a particular focus is specified for your writing:

- With close reference to the language and imagery of the passage, show in what ways it helps to establish important issues in the play.
- Analyse the style and structure of the extract, showing what it contributes to your appreciation of the play's major concerns.

In writing your response, you must of course take account of the precise wording of the task, and ensure you concentrate on each particular point specified. But however the invitation to write about an extract is expressed, it requires you to comment in detail on the language. You should identify and evaluate how the language reveals character, contributes to plot development, offers opportunities for dramatic effect, and embodies crucial concerns of the play as a whole. These 'crucial concerns' are also referred to as the 'themes', or 'issues', or 'preoccupations' of the play.

The following framework is a guide to how you can write a detailed commentary on an extract. Writing a paragraph on each item will help you bring out the meaning and significance of the extract, and show how Shakespeare achieves his effects.

your responses

Paragraph 1: Locate the extract in the play and say who is on stage.

Paragraph 2: State what the extract is about and identify its structure.

Paragraph 3: Identify the mood or atmosphere of the extract.

Paragraphs 4–8:
   Diction (vocabulary)
   Imagery
   Antithesis
   Repetition
   Lists

} These paragraphs analyse how Shakespeare achieves his effects. They concentrate on the language of the extract, showing the dramatic effect of each item, and how the language expresses crucial concerns of the play.

Paragraph 9: Staging opportunities

Paragraph 10: Conclusion

The following example uses the framework to show how the paragraphs making up the essay might be written. The framework headings (in bold) would not, of course, appear in your essay. They are presented only to help you see how the framework is used.

Extract

JULIET   Ay, those attires are best, but, gentle Nurse,
      I pray thee leave me to myself tonight:
      For I have need of many orisons
      To move the heavens to smile upon my state,
      Which, well thou knowest, is cross and full of sin.   5
         [*Enter Juliet's mother, Lady Capulet*]

LADY CAPULET   What, are you busy, ho? need you my help?

JULIET   No, madam, we have culled such necessaries
      As are behoveful for our state tomorrow.
      So please you, let me now be left alone,
      And let the Nurse this night sit up with you,   10
      For I am sure you have your hands full all,
      In this so sudden business.

LADY CAPULET   Good night.
      Get thee to bed and rest, for thou hast need.
         [*Exeunt Lady Capulet and Nurse*]

JULIET   Farewell! God knows when we shall meet again.
      I have a faint cold fear thrills through my veins   15
      That almost freezes up the heat of life:
      I'll call them back again to comfort me.

Nurse! – What should she do here?
My dismal scene I needs must act alone.
Come, vial.   20
What if this mixture do not work at all?
Shall I be married then tomorrow morning?
No, no, this shall forbid it; lie thou there. [*Lays down her dagger.*]
What if it be a poison which the Friar
Subtly hath ministered to have me dead,   25
Lest in this marriage he should be dishonoured,
Because he married me before to Romeo?
I fear it is, and yet methinks it should not,
For he hath still been tried a holy man.
How if, when I am laid into the tomb,   30
I wake before the time that Romeo
Come to redeem me? There's a fearful point!
Shall I not then be stifled in the vault,
To whose foul mouth no healthsome air breathes in,
And there die strangled ere my Romeo comes?   35
Or if I live, is it not very like
The horrible conceit of death and night,
Together with the terror of the place –
As in a vault, an ancient receptacle,
Where for this many hundred years the bones   40
Of all my buried ancestors are packed,
Where bloody Tybalt, yet but green in earth,
Lies fest'ring in his shroud, where, as they say,
At some hours in the night spirits resort –
Alack, alack, is it not like that I,   45
So early waking – what with loathsome smells,
And shrieks like mandrakes' torn out of the earth,
That living mortals hearing then run mad –
O, if I wake, shall I not be distraught,
Environèd with all these hideous fears,   50
And madly play with my forefathers' joints,
And pluck the mangled Tybalt from his shroud,
And in this rage, with some great kinsman's bone,
As with a club, dash out my desp'rate brains?
O look! methinks I see my cousin's ghost   55
Seeking out Romeo that did spit his body

Upon a rapier's point. Stay, Tybalt, stay!
Romeo, Romeo, Romeo! Here's drink – I drink to thee.

(Act 4 Scene 3, lines 1–58)

Paragraph 1: Locate the extract in the play and identify who is on stage
It is the night before Juliet is to be married to Paris. She has already secretly married Romeo, but he has been exiled from Verona. Following a desperate plan made by Friar Lawrence, Juliet has agreed to marry Paris, but is now about to drink a potion which will make her seem as dead. When she is placed in the Capulet tomb, Romeo and the Friar will come to rescue her. Now in her bedroom, Juliet is about to deceive her Nurse and her mother.

Paragraph 2: State what the extract is about and identify its structure
(Begin with one or two sentences identifying what the extract is about, followed by several sentences briefly identifying its structure, that is, the unfolding events and the different sections of the extract.)
   The extract shows Juliet putting Friar Lawrence's dangerous plan into action. She ensures she is left on her own for the night; then, after many fearful thoughts, she drinks the potion. The extract has two sections. First, Juliet deceives her mother and the Nurse. They do not understand the real meaning of her words. Second, she speaks a long soliloquy that reveals both her fears and her determination. She resolves to stab herself if the potion does not work, has doubts about Friar Lawrence's integrity, imagines the horrors of the tomb, but finally, thinking only of Romeo, drinks the 'poison'.

Paragraph 3: Identify the mood or atmosphere of the extract
The mood of the first section is one of dramatic irony. Juliet's words to her Nurse and her mother are full of double meaning. They think she is preparing for marriage to Paris, but she knows she is preparing for a state like death. Juliet's mood in her soliloquy is fearful, even terrified at times, but with moments of great determination.

Paragraph 4: Diction (vocabulary)
The audience recognises that the Nurse and Lady Capulet are unaware of the significance of Juliet's words. 'Gentle Nurse' is ironic because Juliet had only shortly before privately dismissed her as 'Ancient damnation!' for her advice to marry Paris. Neither woman knows what

Juliet really means by her 'state tomorrow': not a joyful bride, but a seemingly dead body. An Elizabethan audience would also see a double meaning in Juliet's use of 'sudden', which then meant 'violent' as well as 'speedy'. In contrast, the words in Juliet's soliloquy unambiguously convey her dread. 'Tomb', 'stifled', 'vault', 'horrible', 'strangled', 'distraught', 'hideous fears' are only a few of the many words concerned with fear and death that create an atmosphere of imagined terrors ahead.

Paragraph 5: Imagery

Juliet's mention that she needs the heavens to smile upon her state is an echo of a major theme of the play, that the lovers are not in control of their own destinies but are 'star-crossed'. Her soliloquy builds up a word picture of the terrors of the Capulet vault. Vivid images help to create its harrowing atmosphere. The tomb is personified as having a 'foul mouth'. The newly buried 'bloody Tybalt' is 'yet but green in earth', and finally rises to vengefully pursue Romeo. The terrifying shrieks in the tomb are imagined in a simile that would have been familiar to Elizabethans: 'shrieks like mandrakes' torn out of the earth'. Mandrakes were plants that were believed to grow below gallows and to shriek as they were pulled up.

Paragraph 6: Antithesis

Antitheses in the soliloquy express the conflict that Juliet feels as she struggles with her emotions. Shakespeare sets her dread against her hope as cold fear 'almost freezes up the heat of life'. Her desire for the 'comfort' of the Nurse is rejected, and she knows she must act 'alone'. Similarly, Juliet rejects marriage, choosing to die by her dagger if the Friar's mixture fails. She expresses her conflicting doubts and certainty about Friar Lawrence's honesty in an antithesis made up of simple words: 'I fear it is, and yet methinks it should not'. Thinking of the terrors of the tomb, her contending emotions are mirrored in oppositions of language: 'foul mouth' is set against 'healthsome air', 'die' against 'live' (which is also set against 'death and night'). But in her final decisive line, she replaces fears of Tybalt with thoughts of Romeo.

Paragraph 7: Repetition

In the soliloquy, immediate repetitions of words express Juliet's rapidly changing moods and thoughts. 'No, no' conveys her determination to die rather than marry. 'Alack, alack' conveys fear. 'Stay, Tybalt, stay!' reveals her desperation. All kinds of emotions may be expressed in her final call to 'Romeo, Romeo, Romeo!'. More subtly, Shakespeare uses repetition to deepen the impression of how her free-flowing imagination torments her with fearful possibilities as she asks 'What if . . .?', 'What if . . .?', How if . . .?', 'O, if . . .?'. Three times in lines 40–3 her repeated 'Where' communicates growing terror with each new horror. Even the repeated 'And' that begins lines 51–3 can help Juliet convey her fear of becoming increasingly deranged.

Paragraph 8: Lists

Shakespeare uses another language technique to enable Juliet to express her growing sense of panic. Her soliloquy can be seen as a long list which accumulates item on item: Will the mixture work? Is the Friar honest? Will she wake in the tomb before Romeo rescues her? Will she go mad with dread? Her imagination builds up a terrifying picture of the 'hideous fears' of the tomb such as 'foul mouth', 'bones', 'bloody Tybalt', 'spirits', 'smells', 'shrieks'. Even her imagining of madness can be seen as a list of actions, beginning with playing with her ancestors' bones and ending with Tybalt's pursuit of Romeo.

Paragraph 9: Staging opportunities

The opening episode offers an opportunity to show the different moods of the three characters. The Nurse and Lady Capulet have no suspicion of Juliet's real intention. They wrongly think that Juliet really is preparing for her wedding tomorrow. But Juliet can make the audience fully aware of the dramatic irony of the situation. She might speak some words (e.g. 'state', 'so sudden business') with a catch in her voice, or with hesitation. The women mistake that style as nervous modesty, but the audience recognise in it her fears about what she must do.

With Juliet left alone on stage, a production can intensify the sense of her utter isolation. For example, dramatic lighting can be used to set her small, vulnerable figure against a vast dark background. Shakespeare's own stage had no lighting facilities, and the actor relied on language, expression and gesture to convey Juliet's extreme anxiety. At the end of her soliloquy she falls on her bed, which on the

Elizabethan stage was in a curtained opening at the back of the stage. Modern productions often have a bed centre stage. Sometimes Juliet speaks almost all her soliloquy seated on the bed. Whatever the staging, two practices usually add to the soliloquy's dramatic effect. First, Juliet remains as still as possible, not using overemphatic physical gestures to illustrate her fears. Second, although she makes the audience fully aware of her emotional distress, she speaks the soliloquy to herself, rather than directly to the audience.

Paragraph 10: Conclusion
The scene reveals how much Juliet has changed since her first appearance in the play. Then, she seemed an obedient, restrained young girl with little to say. Now she displays great strength of character, determination and bravery as she misleads her mother, struggles to master the fears her vivid imagination conjures up, and finally drinks the Friar's dangerous potion. Her action is a crucial turning point in the plot, because her 'death' will bring Romeo back to Verona to die beside her. Juliet's actions and language embody important themes of the play. They show the power of love, and its constant association with death. They suggest the hazards of fortune as she reveals her uncertainties about what she is about to do. Perhaps above all, the agonised movement of her thoughts and feelings reflects the wider conflicts that characterise the whole play.

Reminders

- The framework is only a guide. It helps you to structure your writing. Use the framework for practice on other extracts. Adapt as you feel appropriate. Make it your own.
- Structure your response in paragraphs. Each paragraph makes a particular point and helps build up your argument.
- Focus tightly on the language, especially vocabulary, imagery, antithesis, lists, repetitions.
- Remember that *Romeo and Juliet* is a play, a drama intended for performance. The purpose of writing about an extract is to identify how Shakespeare creates dramatic effect. What techniques does he use?
- Try to imagine the action. Visualise the scene in your mind's eye. But remember there can be many valid ways of performing a scene. Offer alternatives. Justify your own preferences by reference to the language.
- Who is on stage? Imagine their interaction. How do 'silent characters' react to what is said?
- Look for the theatrical qualities of the extract. What guides for actors' movement and expressions are given in the language? Comment on any stage directions.
- How might the audience respond? In Elizabethan times? Today? How might you respond as a member of the audience?
- How might the lines be spoken? Tone, emphasis, pace, pauses? Identify shifting moods and registers. Is the verse pattern smooth or broken, flowing or full of hesitations and abrupt turns?
- What is the importance of the extract in the play as a whole? Justify its thematic significance.
- Are there any 'key words'?
- How does the extract develop the plot, reveal character, deepen themes?
- Offer a variety of interpretations.

Writing an essay

As part of your study of *Romeo and Juliet* you will be asked to write essays, either under examination conditions or for coursework (term papers). Examinations mean that you are under pressure of time, usually having around one hour to prepare and write each essay. Coursework means that you have much longer to think about and produce your essay. But, whatever the type of essay, each will require you to develop an argument about a particular aspect of *Romeo and Juliet*.

Before suggesting a strategy for your essay-writing, it is helpful to recall just what an essay is. Essay comes from the French *essai*: to attempt, or to make a trial. It was originally used by the sixteenth-century French writer Montaigne (whose work Shakespeare certainly read). Montaigne used *essais* to attempt to find out what he thought about particular subjects, such as friendship or cannibals or education. In each essay he used many practical examples to test his response to the topic.

The essays you write on *Romeo and Juliet* similarly require that you set out your thoughts on a particular aspect of the play, using evidence from the text. The people who read your essays (examiners, teachers, lecturers) will have certain expectations of your writing. In each essay they will expect you to discuss and analyse a particular topic, using evidence from the play to develop an argument in an organised, coherent and persuasive way. Examiners look for, and reward, what they call 'an informed personal response'. This simply means that you show you have good knowledge of the play ('informed') and can use evidence from it to support and justify your own viewpoint ('personal').

You can write about *Romeo and Juliet* from different points of view. As pages 89–104 show, you can approach the play from a number of critical perspectives (feminist, political, psychoanalytic, etc.). You can also set the play in its social, literary, political and other contexts, as shown in the section on Contexts. You should write at different levels, moving beyond description to analysis and evaluation. Simply telling the story or describing characters is not as effective as analysing how events or characters embody wider concerns of the play.

In *Romeo and Juliet*, these 'wider concerns' (also called themes, issues, preoccupations – or, more simply, 'what the play is about') include such conflicts as love and hate, youth and age, fate and free will, death and life, light and dark, appearance and reality. In your writing, always give practical examples (quotations, actions) which illustrate the themes you discuss.

How should you answer an examination question or write a coursework essay? The following threefold structure can help you organise your response:

opening paragraph
developing paragraphs
concluding paragraph.

Opening paragraph. Begin with a paragraph identifying just what topic or issue you will focus on. Show that you have understood what the question is about. You probably will have prepared for particular topics. But look closely at the question and identify key words to see what particular aspect it asks you to write about. Adapt your material to answer that question. Examiners do not reward an essay, however well written, if it is not on the question set.

Developing paragraphs. This is the main body of your essay. In it, you develop your argument, point by point, paragraph by paragraph. Use evidence from the play that illuminates the topic or issue, and answers the question set. Each paragraph makes a point of dramatic or thematic significance. Some paragraphs could make points concerned with context or particular critical approaches. The effect of your argument builds up as each paragraph adds to the persuasive quality of your essay. Use brief quotations that support your argument, and show clearly just why they are relevant. Ensure that your essay demonstrates that you are aware that *Romeo and Juliet* is a play, a drama intended for performance and, therefore, open to a wide variety of interpretations and audience response.

Concluding paragraph. Your final paragraph pulls together your main conclusions. It does not simply repeat what you have written earlier, but summarises concisely how your essay has successfully answered the question.

Example

Question: How far do you agree with the view that *Romeo and Juliet* is 'a tragedy of fate'?

The following notes show the 'ingredients' of an answer. In an examination it is usually helpful to prepare similar notes from which you write your essay, paragraph by paragraph. To help you understand how contextual matters or points from different critical approaches might be included, the words 'Context' or 'Criticism' appear before some items. Remember that examiners are not impressed by 'name-dropping': use of critics' names. What they want you to show is your knowledge and judgement of the play and its contexts, and of how it has been interpreted from different critical perspectives.

Opening paragraph
Show that you are aware that the question asks you to show your understanding of 'a tragedy of fate' and then to give reasons for how far you feel that is an adequate description of the play. So include the following points and aim to write a sentence or more on each:

- 'A tragedy of fate' is a critical description of the play – it identifies a genre, a type of play.
- It implies that the disasters in the play have supernatural explanations, and that the characters do not have free will.
- This fatalistic view of the malign influence of fate is justified in references such as 'star-crossed lovers', 'death-marked love', 'the yoke of inauspicious stars'.
- Criticism But there are other ways of looking at the play which reveal that 'a tragedy of fate' is a limited description.

Developing paragraphs
Now write a paragraph on each of a number of different ways in which the play might be described and the causes of the tragedy explained. In each paragraph identify the importance (dramatic, thematic, etc.) of the approach you discuss. Some of the points you might include are given briefly below. At least one aspect of the importance of each is given in brackets, but there are of course others.

- **Criticism** Critics have always been perplexed about the play's genre. (What type of play is *Romeo and Juliet*? In 1621, Robert Burton described it as a 'tragicomedy of love'.)
- **Criticism: traditional** The play could be called a 'tragedy of character', using Aristotle's (and Bradley's) claim that the major character in a tragedy has a 'tragic flaw'. (The disaster is caused by the rash impetuosity and passion of the two young lovers, the angry temperament of Capulet, and the scheming temperament of Friar Lawrence.)
- **Criticism: political and performance** It could be called a 'social tragedy', because Romeo and Juliet are victims of society. (The cause of their death lies in the factions that tear Verona apart, the feud of the Montagues and Capulets. Some modern productions end with the feud still obviously continuing.)
- **Criticism: feminist** It could be called a 'tragedy of patriarchy'. (Male power prohibits genuine love; Capulet treats Juliet as a possession.)
- **Criticism: traditional** It could be called a 'tragedy of accident'. (Bad luck and mischance precipitate the tragedy. Mercutio is killed because of Romeo's intervention; 'O I am fortune's fool'; Friar John is prevented from delivering the letter that would have saved Romeo and Juliet; Juliet wakes too late.)
- **Criticism: psychoanalytic** It might be called a 'death wish tragedy' (following psychoanalytic theory that asserts the desires of love and death are closely linked).
- **Criticism and context** But it may not be a 'tragedy' in the traditional sense. (Charlton called it a 'failed tragedy'; there is much humour in the play; the lovers are young and powerless; their death does not affect the state. Perhaps Brooke's tale, which Shakespeare followed, is a moral tale rather than a tragedy?)

Concluding paragraph
Write several sentences pulling together your conclusions. You might include the following points:

- **Context** The play was described as a tragedy in Quarto and Folio editions.
- **Context and criticism** It can be seen as a tragedy because of the needless waste of young lives.
- But, as shown above, there are many valid alternative ways of

describing the play and explaining the causes of the tragedy. It even has elements of revenge tragedy in it.

- Criticism Much modern criticism is sceptical of fatalistic explanations which imply suffering is inevitable, and humans are powerless to resist. It emphasises social factors which cause tragedy, and which can be challenged and changed.
- So, can only agree to a very limited extent with the description of a 'tragedy of fate'. The play is too complex to be neatly pigeon-holed.

Writing about character

As the section on Critical approaches showed, much critical writing about *Romeo and Juliet* traditionally focused on characters, writing about them as if they were living human beings. Today it is not sufficient just to describe their personalities. When you write about characters you will also be expected to show that they are dramatic constructs, part of Shakespeare's stagecraft. They embody the wider concerns of the play, have certain dramatic functions, and are set in a social and political world with particular values and beliefs. They reflect and express issues of significance to Shakespeare's society – and today's.

All that may seem difficult and abstract. But don't feel overwhelmed. Everything you read in this book is written with those principles in mind, and can be a model for your own writing. Of course you should say what a character seems like to you, but you should also write about how Shakespeare makes him or her part of his overall dramatic design. For example, Shakespeare creates dramatic patterns by making characters equivalent or contrasting in their dramatic functions:

- The Nurse and Friar Lawrence fulfil similar dramatic functions. The Nurse is a surrogate mother-figure for Juliet, just as Friar Lawrence is a father-figure for Romeo. Juliet confides in the Nurse rather than her mother; Romeo confides in the Friar rather than his father.
- Mercutio and the Nurse both mock notions of romantic love. Both are companions and foils to the young lovers, and both leave them isolated: the Nurse by advising Juliet to marry Paris; Mercutio by defending Romeo, only to be killed and thus prompt Romeo to revenge and banishment.

- Benvolio the peacemaker contrasts with Tybalt, always in search of a fight.
- Paris, the Prince and Benvolio have important functions in the design of the play. For Romeo, Paris is the rival suitor, Benvolio the trusted confidant, the Prince a kind of nemesis, sentencing him to banishment. They each help to reveal different aspects of Romeo's character. Each character dramatically 'punctuates' the play. Benvolio's narratives recapitulate the action. The Prince's three appearances have a choric function, and they structure the play, marking its opening, midpoint and end. Paris' appearances have consequences for both Romeo and Juliet, hastening their tragedy.

A different way of thinking about characters is that in Shakespeare's time playwrights and audiences were less concerned with psychological realism than with character types and their functions. That is, they expected and recognised such stock figures of traditional drama as the melancholy young lover (Romeo), the angry father (Capulet), the hot-headed quarreller (Tybalt), the garrulous old servant (the Nurse), and so on. Today, film and television have accustomed audiences to expect the inner life of characters to be revealed. Although Shakespeare's characters do reveal their inmost thoughts and feelings, especially in soliloquy, his audiences tended to regard them as characters in a developing story, to be understood by how they formed part of that story, and by how far they conformed to certain well-known types and fulfilled certain traditional roles.

But there is also a danger in writing about the functions of characters or the character types they represent. To reduce a character to a mere plot device is just as inappropriate as treating him or her as a real person. When you write about characters in *Romeo and Juliet*, you should try to achieve a balance between analysing their personality, identifying the dilemmas they face and placing them in their social, critical and dramatic contexts. That style of writing is found all through this Guide and that, together with the following brief discussions, can help your own written responses to character.

Juliet on her first appearance appears submissive, modest, almost tongue-tied. She has little to say, and appears to respect her mother's authority. But this 13-year-old girl, seemingly conventio'   ⁿd demure, rapidly matures in her meetings with Romeo. S'

Romeo to kiss her only moments after their first meeting, and in their 'balcony' scene she seems to take the lead, speaking twice as many lines as Romeo. She is the one who proposes marriage, and does so the very next day. Faced with her father's demand that she marry Paris, she defies him and then deceives him as she enacts the Friar's plot. Isolated from all support, she shows great courage and resolution in drinking the 'poison'. That same bravery is evident when, unwilling to live without Romeo, she kills herself.

Nineteenth-century critics tended to idealise Juliet and her love for Romeo. They describe her as charmingly innocent, but frank and courageous. They argue that it is her rapid maturity that explains her passion (or, occasionally, they put it down to her being Italian, and so naturally hot-blooded!). Twentieth-century critics are less idealistic. They praise her independence and assertiveness but argue that in creating her character Shakespeare was deliberately challenging conventional assumptions. They point out that Juliet seems unusually precocious: a 13-year-old having sex with a man she's only just met. A typical modern interpretation is that of Sasha Roberts, who uses the Elizabethan view of the 'unruly woman':

> Rather than representing a female ideal Juliet evokes the problematic figure of the unruly woman; the woman who challenges patriarchal dictates and social convention.

Romeo appears first as a stock figure of romance: the moody young lover who is rejected by an unattainable woman. Kiernan Ryan describes him in Act 1 as 'trapped inside the hackneyed role and ossified verse of the Petrarchian lover', seeing himself as the abject slave of a sadistic goddess. Like Orsino in *Twelfth Night*, he seems more in love with love than with an actual person. Granville Barker thought that Shakespeare created him 'by fits and starts' because traces of his early style of speaking are evident throughout the play, together with a progressive deepening of his character. He soon begins to show signs of becoming a tragic figure as he fearfully broods on the future:

> my mind misgives
> Some consequence yet hanging in the stars

> *(Act 1 Scene 4, lines 106–7)*

But there is no doubting his impetuosity. He instan\
marries the next day, and revenges Mercutio's death by ᵢ\
slaying Tybalt. In Friar Lawrence's cell he becomes childₕ\
hysterical, seeming to lose all self-control. In Mantua, learnᵢ\
Juliet's death, he instantly resolves to kill himself in the tomb wᵢₜh
her. Those critics who argue for his growing maturity find their
evidence in his dialogues with Juliet, and in his passionate 'Then I
defy you, stars!' on hearing of her death. His determination to die
beside his beloved Juliet is interpreted as evidence of his unhesitating
commitment to her. Both show their willingness to die for each other.
Whether that really is a sign of maturity is open to argument – and
depends on the society in which you live.

Mercutio is perhaps the most complex character in the play.
Romeo's description of him is incisively accurate: 'A gentleman who
loves to hear himself talk'. He is an intelligent and witty entertainer,
both imaginatively creative and earthily coarse. He mocks love, seeing
it only as sex. His flights of fancy are full of dazzling invention, but
some are judged feverishly neurotic, for example his Queen Mab
speech and his dismissal of foreign sword-fencing techniques in Act 2
Scene 4 ('The pox of such antic, lisping, affecting phantasimes'). He
feels intense friendship for Romeo, and possesses a stern regard for
what he sees as honourable male conduct. His bravery in defending
that honour and his friend results in his death.

Some critics see him as Shakespeare's creation to express male
bonding and to act as Romeo's confidant and foil, as he contrasts
the physical aspects of love with Romeo's idealisation of it. Many
argue, like the playwright and critic John Dryden (1684), that he
becomes such an engaging character that Shakespeare thought it
necessary to kill him off before he completely dominated the play.
Many in the audience feel a sense of loss at his death. But others
challenge that view, arguing that Shakespeare made his early death
dramatically inevitable as the key to the tragedy, spurring Romeo to
revenge.

Friar Lawrence seems the most puzzling character in the play. His
language and actions are open to very different interpretations, as
different stage productions have shown. In some stagings he is
evidently wise and sensible, genuinely concerned to heal the breach
between the Montagues and Capulets. In others he appears devious
and corrupt, or as bumbling and incompetent.

ᴛ ᴉe Friar's problematic nature lies in the gap between his language and his actions. In his first appearance he seems a kind of moral commentator as he speaks of everything having the capacity for good or evil. He advises caution ('Wisely and slow'), and wishes to use the marriage of Romeo and Juliet to bring peace to Verona. But his deeds do not match his words as he always acts hastily. He breaks church law in conducting a secret marriage; proposes a plan to deceive Juliet's parents, from whom he conceals her marriage; risks poisoning Juliet; and abandons her at her moment of greatest need. In short, he continually flouts social norms and subverts conventional authority, and his impulsive actions help cause the death of the lovers.

The **Nurse** is Shakespeare's development of a character type in classical Greek and Roman drama: the garrulous and bawdy servant. She is so engaging that most critics find it impossible to avoid traditional-style character criticism. She seems to have a genuine affection for Juliet, and acts as a go-between for the lovers, helping Juliet deceive her parents. Her earthy, rambling style gives her great stage presence, and prompts critics to be both descriptive and judgemental. Doctor Johnson expresses her personality in a series of antitheses: 'loquacious and secret, obsequious and insolent, trusty and dishonest'.

Right up to the present day, critics have made similarly divided appraisals. They praise the humour the Nurse brings to the play, and accept her frank enjoyment of sexuality and her deflation of romantic love, but they accuse her of moral blindness. She seems such a close and willing ally that her advice to Juliet to marry Paris seems an act of heartless betrayal. It has been described as 'a deceit of the most callous kind'. Frank Kermode labels the Nurse as 'sly' and dismisses her mourning of Juliet merely as imitation of her betters. Such interpretations are highly challengeable, and on stage the Nurse can sometimes appear the most sympathetic character in the play.

Tybalt speaks only 36 lines, but they are remarkably consistent: full of anger and aggression. He seems the stock choleric figure of traditional drama, whose rage and mistaken sense of honour is unrelieved by other, more sympathetic qualities.

Capulet appears first to be genial and hospitable, reminiscing at the party about his youth, and determined to stop Tybalt making trouble. But he proves to be a short-tempered tyrant. He demands absolute obedience from Juliet, and when she refuses he explodes in

Stanley Wells (ed.), *Shakespeare Survey 49: Romeo and Juliet and its Afterlife*, Cambridge University Press, 1996 (contains articles by Davies, Gurr, Snyder, Wells)
Available in or through college libraries. This issue of an annual journal which surveys Shakespeare studies and production concentrates on *Romeo and Juliet*.

Stanley Wells, 'The Challenges of Romeo and Juliet', in *Shakespeare Survey 49*, 1996 (see above)
A discussion of how revisers, actors and directors have addressed challenges of language, character and dramatic construction in the play. Concludes the greatest challenge may be that of genre: What kind of play is it? A romantic tragedy?

Films

At least 23 film versions of the play have been made (and over 60 films adapt its story). A silent version of *Romeo and Juliet* was filmed in France in 1900. Other silent versions were made in Britain, Italy, Germany and America. None of these silent films are available today. The four films of the play listed below are usually obtainable on video or DVD (but distributors sometimes restrict availability in certain countries).

Romeo and Juliet (USA, 1936) Director: George Cukor. Leslie Howard (Romeo), Norma Shearer (Juliet).

Romeo and Juliet (Italy/UK, 1954) Director: Renato Castellani. Laurence Harvey (Romeo), Susan Shentall (Juliet).

Romeo and Juliet (UK, 1968) Director: Franco Zeffirelli. Leonard Whiting (Romeo), Olivia Hussey (Juliet).

William Shakespeare's Romeo + Juliet (USA, 1996) Director: Baz Luhrmann. Leonardo DiCaprio (Romeo), Claire Danes (Juliet).

A video is available of the 1988 BBC television production of the play: Patrick Ryecart (Romeo), Rebecca Saire (Juliet).

Romeo and Juliet has been the inspiration for many film adaptations. Two in particular provide illuminating insights into Shakespeare's play:

West Side Story (USA, 1961) Directors: Robert Wise, Jerome Robbins. Richard Beymer (Tony), Natalie Wood (Maria).

Shakespeare in Love (UK, 1998) Director: John Madden. Joseph Fiennes (Shakespeare), Gwyneth Paltrow (Viola de Lesseps).

Audio books

Four major versions are easily available, in the series produced by:

Naxos: Martin Sheen (Romeo), Kate Beckinsale (Juliet).
Arkangel: Joseph Fiennes (Romeo), Marion Miles (Juliet).
Harper-Collins: Albert Finney (Romeo), Claire Bloom (Juliet).
BBC Radio Collection: Douglas Henshall (Romeo), Sophie Dahl (Juliet).

Romeo and Juliet on the Web

If you type 'Romeo and Juliet Shakespeare' into your search engine, it will find over 80,000 items. Because websites are of wildly varying quality, and rapidly disappear or are created, no recommendation can safely be made here. But if you have time to browse, you may find much of interest.